The Indian Woman

The Indian Woman

CURATED BY
SHOBIT ARYA

EDITED BY
RICHA ANIRUDH

wisdom
tree

Co-editor: Divya S Iyer

Creatives, Photo-research & Editing: Shobit Arya
Copy-editing: Papri Sri Raman, Nikita Singh
Captions: Shobit Arya, Divya S Iyer, Nikita Singh
Design: Kamal P Jammual, Nitin Maheshwari
Review: Nikhilesh Dixit

© Wisdom Tree

First published 2014

ISBN 978-81-8328-355-7

Published by
Wisdom Tree
4779/23, Ansari Road
Darya Ganj, New Delhi-110 002
Ph.: 23247966/67/68
wisdomtreebooks@gmail.com

Printed in India

Contents

Editor's Note

My first lesson in empowerment came from my mother's financial independence. Interestingly, the first earnings of her life happened in the small town of Jhansi in Uttar Pradesh, after she trained at a beauty parlour of one of the illustrious women featured in this book—Shahnaz Husain. It was my mother who dreamt big for me at a time when a lot of parents didn't have such great ambitions for a daughter.

The journey through this book has been an inspiring one for me personally. There are one-of-a-kind personalities like Kiran Mazumdar Shaw, Naina Lal Kidwai, Lata Mangeshkar, who are familiar names in the country and outside. And there are achievers like Surekha Yadav and Chandro Tomar who may not be famous, but their stories leave a lasting impact on the reader. All these women in a way surprised me with their simplicity, humility and accessibility. But I guess these are the very qualities that helped them be where they are and what they are today. I feel that apart from their individual achievements, these women have contributed a great deal in giving a dream to every young girl who wants to make a place for herself in this world.

I strongly believe that behind every successful woman, there is family—parents, spouse and children—and friends. That's the biggest strength for her and she doesn't mind accepting it. Another striking characteristic in several stories of these women icons is their small town background—they grew up in humble, middle-class homes. What really impressed me about these women is that none of them ever sought any concession for being a woman. They all firmly believed that once you are out there in the professional world, your gender really doesn't matter. And this is one message that all young women should certainly take from these icons. If you want to be treated equally, don't ask for favours.

This book, for me, is more about Indian women at large rather than the few stories included here. When I commute between my workplace and home, one sight always catches my attention. Simple girls, modest women waiting at the bus stops—I look at them and get drawn into thoughts—here is an Indian woman who would have finished all household chores, cooking, cleaning, sending kids to school, before leaving for her work. In the evening, she will not be able to relax at home because dinner will have to be cooked, children's homework will have to be supervised and many endless, thankless jobs to be done. This is the true Indian woman, each one of whom is an icon in her own right. So, I dedicate this book to that woman standing at the bus stop, in hope and courage...

—Richa Anirudh

right
Indian women have several firsts to their credit. Women officers from the Indian police had the distinction to form the first all-women UN peace keeping mission in Liberia in 2007. They have received praise for their efficient and just handling of the delicate situation.

Introduction

Her compassion unfathomable, her determination unbeatable and her conviction impregnable—if we were to assimilate the pith and core of the timelessness of Indian civilisation, one factor that would shine through brighter than most others, would be the strength of the Indian woman.

Today, as the women of India stand tall on the shoulders of ancestors who worshipped, idolised and respected womanhood, they certainly have a sublime legacy to be proud of. All things eternal—Mother Goddess, all things enduring—Mother Earth, all things unwavering—Mother India, and all things unconditional—a mother's love, have always been etched intricately on this nation's consciousness.

Let's begin from the beginning. Shakti—the all-powerful divine feminine is believed to be the personification of cosmic energy, the manifest; and Shiva—the supreme God, the all encompassing consciousness, the unmanifest. The confluence of energy and consciousness, the female and the male that created the universe, and that which lives on in every human being, is delicately woven with the threads of divinity in the Shakti-Shiva constructs. This tradition of unity of the feminine with the masculine continues with the legends of Sita-Ram and Radha-Krishna, the fact that the feminine is mentioned before the masculine reflects her undisputed status. That the land of a million gods and goddesses accepted into its fold, cultures and religions from faraway regions to seamlessly transition into the secular, plural and liberal nation India is today, can also to an extent be attributed to the faith and fervency of Indian women.

India has been witness to many a heroine who engendered change and transformation of the society through her history. If India's intellectual rigour has defined her through the times—with the Vedas and Upanishads laying the foundation, women seers like Gargi and Maitreyi contributed important verses to these ancient scriptures. Mystics and poetesses like Andal, Khana, Lal Ded and Meera Bai further enriched the country's spiritual heritage with their perennial works. And it wasn't just India's cultural ethos which gained immensely from their contribution. The hands that wielded the quill equally ably wielded the sword. Rani Durgavati, Razia Sultan, Jijabai and Rani Lakshmi Bai proved that when the need arises, a woman's valour can match and surpass any man's. Their lives inspired and continue to inspire millions of women in India as well as rest of the world, a testimony to which is borne by stories in this book as well. The likes of Rani Ahilya Bai Holkar and Rani Rudrama Devi, with their just and efficient administration, laid the foundations of the modern

right
Faith and secularism remain deep rooted in the hearts of Indian women. They play a prime role in maintaining the spiritual and liberal fabric of the country. A woman enters Swaminarayan Temple in Bhuj, Gujarat, where the newly constructed magnificent temple—adjacent to the main temple—has an assembly hall that can cater to 1,000 female devotees.

nation state of India, which has had a woman prime minister, a woman president and several women chief ministers. Several women freedom fighters and leaders stood unshakable in the face of adversity during the struggle for Independence—Sarojini Naidu, Kalpana Dutta, Vijayalakshmi Pandit and Aruna Asaf Ali to name some of the most unforgettable of them. One cannot but pay tribute to these women of substance, whose contributions have moulded the character of the quintessential Indian woman.

Even as we delight in the glory of the past, we cannot overlook the concerns of the present. The universal challenges of gender bias, unequal opportunities and lack of security have often impeded the progress of India's women on their road to empowerment. The turn of events in India in recent times has seen strengthening of the voices against such malice. Several reformative measures are being amped up, both by the state as well as society, setting in motion a wave of affirmative action in support of women. The recently instituted Bharatiya Mahila Bank (a financial institution exclusively manned by, and catering to the needs of women) in a bid to financially empower the Indian woman, the numerous schemes and programmes such as Janani Suraksha Yojana, SABLA etc. implemented by the Government of India in order to protect and nurture the girl child, the amended legislative measures to enhance safety of women in the country—all work in harmony with the endeavours of India's women to realise their dreams.

And the new dreamers do not need to look too far for inspiration. Four Indian women were featured in the Fortune's 50 Most Powerful Women in Business in 2013—the maximum from any single developing country on the list. Not to forget the 'Iron Lady of India'—Indira Gandhi, who was voted as the greatest woman of the past 1,000 years in a global poll conducted by BBC News Online in 1999. As Indian women continue to conquer grids and gorges across the globe, it would be imperative to learn from the lives of those who have overcome extreme challenges and risen to enviable positions. They not only show us the way to ascension, but also add to the repository of wisdom that the modern Indian woman stands to gain from. Entrepreneurs and entertainers, activists and accountants, scientists and sculptors, economists and ecologists—the professions may be unending and so would be the list of illustrious Indian women who have left an indelible impression on the nation and

from l to r
Sunita Williams, Navi Pillay, Indra Nooyi and Kalpana Chawla. Illustrious women of Indian origin have been great flag bearers of Indian enterprise and culture across the globe.

UN HIGH COMMISSIONER FOR HUMAN RIGHTS

the world. Several stories of such Indian women have been captured in this book. *The Indian Woman*, thus, offers readers what India is best known for—a symphony of distinct characters and unique stories; a potpourri of intense struggles and astonishing achievements; a thali that scintillates the senses and satiates the soul.

The book opens with the fascinating journeys of some exceptional Indian women who have pioneered growth and development of the nation, ironing out gender differences and venturing successfully into seemingly impossible and unchartered territories. The individual excellence of each of these gems remains unparalleled as she proclaims *I am Every Woman*. The second section assays the lives of women who have demonstrated extraordinary skills, setting a trail-blazing record in spheres often deemed unsuitable for women. They have led the way for other women to march ahead, echoing to the strums of *Every Woman is Her*. No bouquet would be complete without the scent of fresh blooms, and no book without the fragrance of remembrances. The third section offers a glimpse into the lives of ten historic Indian women who continue to live in the memories of the nation—*She is in Every Woman*.

Indian women have not limited themselves to conventional contours and geographical coordinates. Today, we are proud of the Indian women abroad who have not just excelled in their adopted countries, but have been great ambassadors for their country of origin as well. The woman of courage—astronaut Kalpana Chawla as well as Sunita Williams; of compassion—United Nation Human Rights Commission chairperson Navi Pillay; of enterprise—Pepsi Co CEO Indra Nooyi; of excellence—economist Padma Desai; of science—Sunetra Gupta; of arts—Patricia Maria Rozario; of activism—Amina Cachalia; of politics—Kamla Persad-Bissessar; of literature—Jhumpa Lahiri and of elegant normality—the woman toiling for her family away from her homeland—she is the face of India abroad as she holds the luminous torch of the nation high. The healthy exchange of human resources beyond the barriers of nationality has gifted our country too, in equally sound measures. Ida Sophia Scudder, Annie Besant, Nellie Sengupta and Miraben are a few names not to be missed while remembering the birth of independent India. The book wraps up with homage to Mother Teresa, whose immortal spirit of love and compassion continues to define the Indian Woman. The journey of 'The Indian Woman' begins here.

—Shobit Arya, Divya S Iyer

I
AM
EVERY
WOMAN

Fascinating journeys of
some of the most acclaimed women of India.
In their own words.

Brew Your Dreams

Kiran Mazumdar Shaw

As a starry-eyed young girl, charmed by a salubrious city and the comfort of a caring household, I grew up in the science capital of India—Bengaluru, imbibing scientific curiosity from the atmosphere around me. Somewhere within, I was embarrassed by my father's profession, all because he worked for the liquor industry! He was a 'brewer'. His reprimand remains the philosophy of my life, his words ring loud in my ears even today, 'Do not be judgmental on any matter with half knowledge'. My father was a man way ahead of his times, and taught me to look at life just the way my brothers did. He was very troubled by society's attitude towards women and wanted me to challenge it by pursuing a professional career. It was he who inculcated in me a scientific interest in beer brewing, and helped me change my disconcerted mind at the prospect of taking up brewing as a career.

I certainly got my spunk from my Australia days, where I was the only girl in the class for the master-brewer course at Ballarat University near Melbourne. But once I returned to my country, I was in for a huge shock. I discovered that existing breweries were happy to engage me as a consultant to troubleshoot for them, but not willing to hire me as a brew master, just because I was a woman. The rebel in me almost gave up, and I decided to pursue opportunities outside of India. I was about to move to Scotland to take up a brewing job, when fate intervened in the form of Leslie Auchincloss, the founder of an Irish biotech company, Biocon Biochemicals. Leslie wanted to set up a company in India, and wanted me to be his Indian partner, after getting my reference from Ballarat University.

After great persuasion, I agreed, and in 1978, I set up Biocon India as a joint venture with Biocon Biochemicals of Ireland, with an initial investment of just ₹10,000. I was twenty-five years old. The most amusing encounters I had in those days were with my prospective employees who, during interviews, would actually 'reverse interview' me in order to allay their apprehensions regarding their job security of working in a start-up company founded by a woman. The banks wouldn't fund a woman entrepreneur, the suppliers from whom I had to procure raw-materials for my production process would insist that I send a man to negotiate.

After one year's toil in a rented garage, I started manufacturing papain—a plant proteolytic enzyme derived from the latex of the papaya fruit, which is plentiful in India. This successful debut encouraged me to take many more risks in business, and all that I had saved in the first year was invested into a twenty-acre property. I was often asked why such a small company needed so much land, but I had the courage to defy the sceptics and dream big.

Today, we have a large drug substance facility as well as Biocon's corporate offices on the same land and we also have an additional campus, spread over nearly 100 acres, housing over 7,000 employees, which is now the largest biotech hub in Asia. Yet, I still sit at the same desk that I used in 1978 when I set up the first manufacturing plant at the Biocon campus. I am sentimental about it. From this desk, I set out to shape Biocon as the largest enzymes company of India. Along this journey, I received various recognitions, including the Padma Shri in 1989, I was probably the youngest woman to receive this prestigious national award, and many more followed.

In 1998, when the Irish company underwent change of ownership, I decided to take complete charge of Biocon India and bought back the shares, with my husband's help. Having established leadership status in enzymes, we set out for a larger goal. I wanted to make a global impact by making a difference to thousands of patients worldwide. We embarked on a journey of becoming an innovation-led biopharmaceutical company, and developed a business model that leveraged our strengths in fermentation technology. Thus, we successfully became one of the leading statins producers of the world and also entered the area of bio-similars.

Biocon is the only company in the world to make pichia fermentation technology-based recombinant human insulin, which was launched in India as Insugen in 2004. The year 2004 was also very significant for us, as Biocon became the first biotech company to be listed on the stock exchange, and also crossed a major milestone, achieving an evaluation of US$ 1.1 billion, on day one.

As Asia's largest producer of insulin, we are also pursuing development of oral insulin, currently in phase II of clinical trials. We are confident about taking this to market, as we know it will simplify diabetes management in a big way. We have a strong research

left
Kiran Mazumdar Shaw launches Basalog, a long-acting human insulin analog for type 1 and type 2 diabetes, in Bengaluru. Biocon has set up its first overseas bio-pharma manufacturing and research facility in Malaysia.

services business, focused on integrated drug discovery and development through our subsidiary Syngene. Biocon now operates in over eighty-five countries and does business of around US$ 500 million annually. But my emphasis is on rewriting the equation between affordability and accessibility for the billions of patients who are denied health care in India and elsewhere. I would love to see one of our novel drugs make a huge difference to patients all over the world. In a modest attempt to care for those patients afflicted by the horrible disease of cancer, I started the 1,400-bedded cancer care centre in Bengaluru. I was devastated when a close friend of mine was diagnosed with breast cancer and realised how gruelling an experience it is to go through an illness of that kind and how, even affluent families grapple with managing money to treat cancers that require highly expensive biologics, which have to be imported into India even today.

Destiny has always stoked me to raise myself from the bottom of a pit, from time to time in my life. My mother is a cancer survivor and so is my husband, who was diagnosed with cancer a few years ago but has, thankfully, recovered. During these trying times, I learnt so much about psycho-oncology and the critical role it plays in helping people deal with the killer disease. It is so acutely absent in therapy in this country. There is such a great need for it. The world has to care for every patient that needs a cure. Through the Biocon Foundation that was formed in 2005, we are also engaged in community-based healthcare services in the rural areas of Karnataka, apart from offering health insurance coverage to over 1,00,000 people in rural communities every year.

I grew up being very apologetic about my country; a country of primitive technology and status-quo approach to development—that was the wide-spread perception prevalent in those times. So, I felt a strong urge to create something that would be a

piece of new India; an advanced nation for the next generation, which would be proud of its country's standing. The India that I see now is in stark contrast to the notion prevalent two decades ago; as I witness a microcosm of India in my company every day, with a lot of cutting edge research, innovation and scientific processes churning out immeasurable benefits to mankind; where a woman entrepreneur is no longer a rare breed. But I do feel that when it comes to providing equal opportunity to everyone, regardless of gender and other discrimination, we still have a long way to go.

As a child, I was fascinated with the idea of becoming a doctor, and was heart-broken when I could not make it to a medical school. But life—through its winding, intriguing alleys—has taken me back to the science of medicine, though not as a doctor, but as a researcher. Today, I get to interact and work very closely with the medical fraternity and it feels as if life has indeed come a full circle.

The urge to achieve, combined with fearless action imbued with common sense, is my prescription for any young girl who asks me, 'How can I grow up to be like you?' Listen to the powerful voice from within, enable reinventing yourself at a young age itself and never cease to evolve into a better person so that you break free, dream big, become large-hearted, and build something memorable to make the world a better place for everyone to live in.

Of all the robes that I don in my professional life, as an entrepreneur, an innovator, an engaged citizen, a hearty friend or a warm colleague, the one that makes a world of difference is the compassionate giver in me. I have pledged to give away three fourth of my wealth to those in need of affordable healthcare and work tirelessly to improve cancer care in India, through our highly dedicated, talented and enterprising team at Biocon: India's largest biopharma company focused on affordable innovation.

—with Divya S Iyer

A panoramic shot of the synthetic chemistry Lab at Syngene, Bengaluru. Syngene, which is a custom research and development facility, is one of Biocon's two subsidiaries. The other is Clinigene, a clinical research organisation.

Bringing Stories to Life

Bhanu Athaiya

'This is too good to be true,' I uttered these words in a daze after I received the award for 'Best Costume Design' for Richard Attenborough's *Gandhi*, at the 55th Academy Awards on 11 April 1983 at the Dorothy Chandler Pavilion in Los Angeles. I shared the win with John Mollo, my British counterpart. It was the first ever win by an Indian.

A very special memory, but in my heart, the earliest, most vivid and treasured memories are of my parents. My father Annasaheb Rajopadhye, who combined tradition with a passion for the arts and my mother Shantabai who, with her indomitable spirit led a principled life, setting an example for her children.

My father was and remains my deepest inspiration. He painted and was an avid photographer, who developed his own pictures. I cleaned the brushes for him and also kept time in the darkroom. These were my first baby steps into the world of artistic expression. He noticed my interest in art and engaged a special teacher who taught me paper craft, when I was all of eight! He introduced me to Western cinema. I remember Greta Garbo in *Queen Christina* and Charlie Chaplin in *Gold Rush*. I even played the part of a prince in *Mohini*, a movie my father made with Usha Mantri.

I was only nine when my father passed away and it was my mother who stood by the seven of us, the eldest just fifteen, the youngest still a baby. It was the 1930s, not an easy time for a woman, but she never let herself get overwhelmed and lived her life with courage and dignity. She trusted each one of us, encouraging us to follow our dreams. When my teacher, Shashikishore Chavan, asked her to allow me to apply to the Sir JJ College of Art, she agreed.

I was seventeen, a young girl in a big city. It was pre-Independence Mumbai, but because of my mother's confidence in me, I felt empowered. I wanted to be independent and was very lucky to get a break as an illustrator in the magazine, *Fashion & Beauty*. The launch of *Eve's Weekly* followed and I shifted and began contributing two pages of fashion illustrations. All this while, I was also studying, finally graduating with a Gold medal and a fellowship. I was also a member of the Progressive Artists' Group.

Maybe I could have had a career in art, but my editor opened a boutique and soon it was being frequented by film personalities. Kamini Kaushal was the first to commission me to design clothes for her and this led to costume designing, what one calls *haute couture*. *Aas* in 1953 was followed by *Shahenshah* and I was on my way to becoming India's first costume designer. Nargis, who was an early patron, one day took me to R K Studios where *Shri 420* was already on the floors. I was asked to design costumes for Nadira, who was playing the vamp in the movie. I succeeded in making her look glamorous and unconventional and went on to do several films with Raj Kapoor. Another very famous director and actor was Guru Dutt and I was associated with some of his most beautiful films like *CID*, *Pyaasa*, *Kaagaz ke Phool* and several others. The youth of a newly independent India was searching for an identity, a way to stay true to their roots and still be contemporary. Films were defining fashion trends, it was wonderful to see glimpses of what I designed on the streets, but I did not become a household name in fashion designing. I was a costume designer, a technician, and a craftsperson—that was and remains my identity.

When I look back at a lifetime of work, *Gandhi* stands out as one of the most challenging assignments. This movie remains very close to my heart because Mahatma Gandhi had a firsthand influence on me; as a child I heard talk of the freedom struggle. As I grew up, people had taken to wearing *khadi*, it was a movement that was overtaking our lives—no amount of research could have helped understand that time as living in it had.

Dolly Thakore was the casting director and she asked Simi Garewal to contact me. I did not even possess a phone! Simi came to my workshop and overrode any doubts I expressed, saying, 'This is an important assignment and a great opportunity to show your talent. I am fixing an appointment, wear something nice and bring your biodata with you.' The auditions were being held in Sea Rock Hotel. The interview

left
Bhanu Athaiya holds her Oscar statuette, after being awarded the Academy Award in 1983 for the 'Best Costume Design' for *Gandhi*. Although India had received three nominations before, this was the country's first Oscar win.

page 9
A beautiful sketch in the working stage by Bhanu Athaiya, who had begun her career as a freelance fashion illustrator. In 2010, her book *The Art of Costume Design*, in which she shares her passion for creativity in design and takes the readers through her enthralling journey, was released in India.

page 10
Indian women are adept at creating a symphony between tradition and modernity. A handicrafts expert working with Madhya Pradesh state tourism department showcases the movements of a handloom weaving machine at the Mrignayanee Emporium in Ahmedabad.

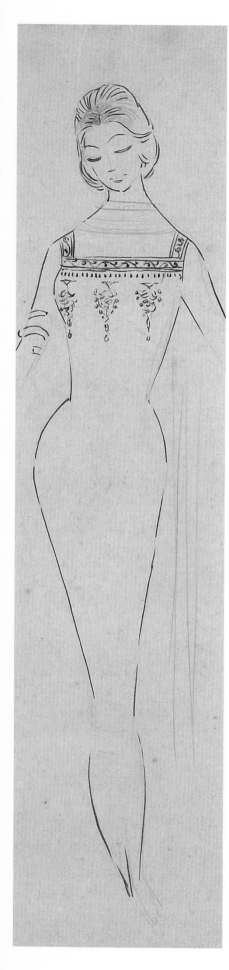

was the easy part; Sir Attenborough interviewed me and, in fifteen minutes, announced he had found his designer.

By this time, I had been working for about twenty-five years in the film industry, but had never dealt with such a large canvas—fifty years of Mahatma Gandhi's life in various locations, including Dandi and South Africa where Gandhi was young and covering a span of time as he changed over the years. There were sequences where hundreds of people in period costumes had to be used. To get everything right, I carried out extensive research, I worked from photographs and spent days in museums all over the country. In the film, Jawaharlal Nehru's outfits are probably the most authentic, since Indira Gandhi made it possible for me to actually see his clothes, which had been packed away and preserved. I could examine the cut, feel the fabric and inspect the 'fall'. His attire also transforms drastically in the course of the film; he starts out wearing Saville Row suits after his return from England, but once he comes under the influence of Mahatma Gandhi, he dons a dhoti, kurta and waistcoat and finally moves to *sherwani* and *churidar pyjama*.

All the hard work paid off. One of the best compliments I received was from Phyllis Dalton, the costume designer for *Dr Zhivago*, who met me and said, 'Out there in LA, the producers think that India comes all ready-made. All you need to do is come here with a camera and go out and shoot. All thanks to you.' A compliment I cherish because it points to the fact that sometimes, blending into a story is more difficult than standing out. The movie led to my becoming a voting member of the Academy and I receive the Oscar ballot paper every year.

Each day brought something new with it, new stories, characters and new challenges. *Lekin*, an unusual film directed by Gulzar, got me the National Award for Best Costume Design in 1990. In 2001, I got a chance to do the costumes of *Lagaan*. It was wonderful to execute the entire look from the villagers of Champaner, to the British regiment, English civilians and even cricket costumes. Ashutosh Gowarikar, the director, gave me the complete script and three months in which to execute the costumes, a rare and very welcome gesture. I received the National Award for *Lagaan* at the hands of former President APJ Abdul Kalam. The year 2004 saw me designing for another patriotic film, *Swades*, where I received compliments for Shah Rukh Khan's look. In 2009, I received the Filmfare Lifetime Achievement Award. I clothed some of the best actors and actresses and did not have any favourites. But if I had to choose the one actress I most loved designing for, it would be Waheeda Rehman. Her innate grace would take over a piece of clothing and she'd make it her own, her demeanor would change, her body would sway in a sari and swing in line with a ghagra!

I loved my work and was passionate about the research that went into bringing a character to life. I was working with the best names in the industry, directors who were very serious about their craft, spending hours discussing their ideas, but giving me my space to finally give shape to a finished look for a character. As Richard Attenborough wrote in the foreword to my book, 'Costume designing is about giving an actor absolute confidence in the character he or she is to inhabit; about creating a mood and transporting the audience to a different era or place.

It required organisation, artistry, discipline, expertise, imagination and more often than not, many hours of research.'

I had a fairytale childhood in the princely state of Kolhapur. On my way to school, I would often see horses and elephants in magnificent processions, the Maharaja in the centre. To grow up and spend a lifetime working with directors and actors, bringing stories to life on the big screen, was an unbelievable journey and not any less than a fairytale! My first job, cleaning my father's paint brushes, was where it all began, and today as I sit in my workshop, surrounded by his paintings and my sketches, I know he would have been very proud.

—As told to Harman Kaur

Nature, the Beautician

Shahnaz Husain

Entrepreneurship stems from the independence of one's spirit. It is encouraging to see that women in India have begun unleashing this spirit in recent times, as a result of which, our society is enriched by a growing number of empowered women entrepreneurs. I consider myself privileged to be one of the early members of this progressive movement. In fact, when I look back, I feel that much more than I have ever dreamt of has come true. The Shahnaz Husain Group of Companies based on Ayurveda, the vision of my dreams, is a reality today that straddles the international cosmetic market. The company operates in more than hundred countries, with a global network of franchise salons, spas, shops, beauty training academies and direct product distributors for our range of four hundred organic formulations for beauty and health care.

I had a fairytale childhood. I was fortunate to have a caring father, Chief Justice N U Beg, who put me through schooling in a convent at Allahabad and instilled in me a love of poetry and English literature. He also imbued in me the right combination of traditional values and progressive ideas. I learnt to love and respect the rich heritage of India.

I will never forget that while I was in school, Mother Bernard called my father and said, 'While all the children go to church early morning on Sunday, your daughter is sleeping. Please send a teacher to educate her in Islam, because she does not know any religion.' My father responded, 'Since my child doesn't know any religion, please teach her yours.' From that day, my attitude towards religion changed. I realised that there is no *personal god*. There is a spiritual power that rules the universe and that is what is termed as religion or God. After that, I attended church every Sunday.

I was married at sixteen and had a daughter within the year. But I knew that I was not meant to be a housewife. Soon, the boredom and monotony of routine set in. I suddenly realised the hard-hitting truth of the words I once wrote, 'Let not my life be a series of days and nights, of hopes and sighs; so that when I die, I will close my eyes and say, it was all worthwhile.'

I had always been interested in beauty. Soon, I had the opportunity to learn about it in greater detail in London, Paris, Germany, Denmark and New York. Then, at twenty-seven, my husband was posted as head of Foreign Trade with the State Trading Corporation of India in Tehran. I needed money for higher education. I could not speak Persian, so a job was not easy. I was a prolific writer. I finally got an opening as Beauty Editor of *Iran Tribune*, a magazine. I was asked to give them 500 words a week. I submitted 10,000 words a week! I wrote on every subject under the sun, from prose to poetry. I wrote under several pennames. Soon, I was running the entire magazine; only the cover was designed by the press. My confidence soared, so did my income. But my fingers suffered from continuous punching of the typewriter keys.

I stayed on in Tehran for three years and continued typing—fingers bleeding, hands bandaged. I returned to India three years later with wounds, but had saved enough money to pay an advance deposit for five years for my beauty courses in six countries.

It was while studying abroad that I realised there was something terribly wrong with the beauty business. The world was struggling under the harmful effects of chemicals and something needed to be done to provide a harmless alternative. I then began thinking about going back to nature and finding treatments that were safe and had no risks to skin, hair or eyes.

I wanted to formulate natural products from herbs. I had the traditional knowledge that, we in India have always been using nature produce like turmeric and cucumber. And when I looked towards nature, I did find a better alternative. The study of Ayurveda finally convinced me that it could offer the ideal answers to all the synthetic ills.

I had two options, either to start a private clinic for cures as an answer to a human need and basic desire to look attractive, or to enter the market. I chose the former and started a herbal clinic, where I could solve individual problems. I knew I would earn less, but I would achieve satisfaction. I borrowed ₹35,000 from my father and converted a verandah of my house into a clinic, by adding a roof. That is how it all began.

Now, after forty-three years, we have a chain of about four hundred franchise clinics in India and abroad, under the Shahnaz Herbal banner. I entered the retail market only about two decades ago.

left
Shahnaz Husain at the World Trade Fair at Pragati Maidan, New Delhi. She has been invited to several prestigious institutions like MIT, London School of Economics and University of Oxford to share her experiences.

I achieved unprecedented success in the Festival of India in 1981, where our sales broke the Selfridges' record. The next day, the *Daily Telegraph* had a headline saying, 'Herbal Hell Breaks Loose at Selfridges'. This was followed by a more positive BBC television interview titled 'Brand India rules the Cosmetic World'. In an interview abroad, I was told that I have a superiority complex about India and her herbal heritage. I answered, 'I have no complex; we *are* superior.'

When the world had no chemicals, India always had herbs. Chemicals came centuries later. Since our entry into the international market, our chain of clinics and outlets has extended rapidly, to every corner of the globe.

The Government of India featured me in a television series for the United Nations' established consortium, called, 'Woman of the Decade' and later awarded me the coveted Padma Shri. Little did I know that several international awards and recognition would follow. They included the Success Magazine's 'World's Greatest Woman Entrepreneur' award in 1996, Woman of the Millennium Award in USA etc. I recently received three awards in London for Outstanding Ayurvedic Innovation, including one at the British Parliament. It gives me a sense of pride, because I had a burning desire to put India on the world beauty map and have the Indian flag flying high in the cosmetic capitals of the world.

We tried to be innovative in our communication and reaching out as well. Instead of advertising, I relied on the fact that a satisfied client was the best advertisement. In fact, I was invited by the Harvard Business School to speak on how I established an international brand without commercial advertising.

I have always wanted to encourage the Indian housewife to have a career and attain financial independence, because I think it makes all the difference. I, therefore, set up our beauty school, the Woman's World International, now known as The Shahnaz Husain International Beauty Academy, and followed a comprehensive syllabus. This was more than thirty-five years ago and at that time, only apprenticeship training was available in beauty. I encouraged housewives to learn beauty and open their own salons in their own homes, under the Shahnaz Herbal banner. I thought this would ensure that they could pursue a career without having to leave home. I also started Shasight for the visually impaired and Shamute, a free training school for the speech and hearing impaired.

I have had many valued customers and celebrities endorsing my products, but the one that I value most even today is when our former Prime Minister, Indira Gandhi, wanted me to formulate a moisturiser for her, and thus 'Shamoist' was born. One of the most touching moments in my life was when my daughter Nelofar unveiled the book titled *Flame: The Story of my Mother*, depicting my life in a way only a daughter can.

The measure of success I have achieved in life is not according to what I have earned, but how much happiness and self-confidence I have been able to instil in others. If one is true to oneself, success will follow. I have believed that it is not what you want in life—what really matters is how badly you want it. I have also believed that it is the quality and not quantity of life spent that is important. For others, a good life may mean living for a hundred years. For me, I live a lifetime between the rising and the setting of the sun. I would not have it any other way. I have dedicated my life to India's herbal heritage. Let the future be the witness. I have always felt, 'One life is not enough'.

right (top)
A young woman in a Yoga pose (Asana). Yoga and Meditation are integral to well-being in the Indian tradition which has viewed health from a holistic angle since time immemorial.

right (bottom)
The cosmetic and beauty industry in India has seen some major women players, who have established themselves and provide ample employment opportunities to women.

Reinventing Growth

Sunita Narain

It is always difficult to write about 'myself'. As a journalist, my work is to explore what is happening in our world and find the nuggets of hope that bring change. But when I think about what has defined my own journey, it is clear that it was inspiration of the people in my life that gave me the drive and, in fact, the passion to make a difference.

I grew up in a privileged world of books and knowledge. My grandfather, Sri Krishna, was an eminent journalist whose house was filled with books and papers. My mother, Usha Narain, shared her father's interest in plants and gardening. His house, located in what is now New Delhi's busy Jantar Mantar area, was a bundle of plants and books. I think back, and I realise that my own desire to work to protect the natural and the 'lived' environment and to use knowledge as a tool to bring change came naturally to me.

I was only eight years old, when my father, Raj Narain, passed away when on a business trip to Europe. My mother was left with four daughters to bring up, me being the eldest. Against many odds, she took up my father's work. Over the next many years, she provided all of us with the best of education and everything else that makes life so delightful. Today, when people ask me how I face difficult situations at work, I think only of the challenges and strength it took my mother to bring up four daughters. She gives me the inspiration to do much more with my own life—it would be nothing less than a disservice to her life to do anything less.

When I was passing out of high school in 1980, environment was hardly an issue of any public concern. It was certainly not a profession that my friends thought of joining. This was also the time when environmental issues had reached the global arena. In 1972, the world conference on environment had been held in Stockholm. Indira Gandhi, the then Prime Minister of India, was one of the few developing world leaders who attended it. It was also in the 1970s, that news of a movement in the remote Himalayas, where women had hugged trees to protect them from woodcutters, was doing the rounds. The Chipko Movement, as it was known, brought consciousness of how environment was important for the very poor.

This is how my work on environmental issues began. While in school, I happened to go to a conference being held at the Gandhi Peace Foundation in Delhi to discuss this movement. There I met two other fellow students—from different Delhi schools—who had similar interests. We joined hands to form a student organisation in the field of environment, called Kalpvriksh—the tree of life.

Our work together took us to visit the women of the Chipko Movement. As we travelled through the Himalayas, I began to see the connection between livelihoods and environment.

A few years later, I met Anil Agarwal, who had just founded the Centre for Science and Environment (CSE) and was beginning work on an ambitious project called the State of India's Environment (SOE). As I began working with Anil, the connections I had made in the Himalayas began to provide stark lessons—environment is about development. For millions in India, environment is not a luxury—a matter to worry about after they are prosperous. Environment is about survival. People depend on the environment—land, water, forests—and without this, poverty is exacerbated. I learnt that rejuvenating the natural asset was the way for economic growth. This gave me the reason I needed to pursue this work. It was the way forward for India's economic growth.

Those early years with Anil taught me a lot. He wanted to understand how this natural regeneration could take place. So we travelled to the villages where communities had come together to build a green future. There I saw the difference that good management of forest and water could bring to people's lives. Anil and I quickly learnt to look beyond trees, at ways to deepen democracy, so these commons—in India, forests are mostly owned by government agencies, but it is the poor who use them—could be regenerated. It became clear that without community participation, planting trees was not possible. For people to be involved, the rules of engagement had to be respected. To be respected, the rules had to be fair.

left
Sunita Narain enlightening young minds at the Asian University for Women. She has worked tirelessly towards environment conservation, for which the Indian Government awarded her the Padma Shri in 2005. She is also a recipient of the World Water Prize for her work on rainwater harvesting.

This initiation helped me understand the challenges of climate change as well. In the same period, data released by a prestigious US research institution completely convinced our then Environment Minister that it was the poor who contributed substantially to global warming—they did 'unsustainable' things like growing rice or keeping animals. Anil and I were pulled into this debate when a flummoxed chief minister of a hill state called us. He had received a government circular that asked him to prevent people from keeping animals. 'How do I do this?' he asked us. 'Do the animals of the poor really disrupt the world's climate system?'

We were equally foxed. It seemed absurd. Our work told us that the poor were victims of environmental degradation. Here they were now, complete villains. How?

With this question, we embarked on our climate research journey. We began to grasp climate change issues, and quickly learnt that there wasn't much of a difference between managing a local forest and the global climate. Both were common property resources. What was needed, most of all, was a property rights framework, which encouraged cooperation. One, the world needed to differentiate between the emissions of the poor—from subsistence paddy or animals—and that of the rich, from, say, cars. Survival emissions are not and can not be equivalent to luxury emissions.

Two, it was clear that managing a global common meant cooperation between countries. As a stray cattle or goat is likely to chew up saplings in the forest, any country could blow up the agreement if it emitted beyond what the atmosphere could absorb. Cooperation was only possible—and this is where our forests experience came in handy—if benefits were distributed equally. We then developed the concept of per capita entitlements—each nation's share of the atmosphere—and used the property rights of entitlement to set up rules of engagement that were fair and righteous. We said that countries using less than their share of the atmosphere could trade their unused quota, and this would give them the incentive to invest in technologies that would not increase their emissions. But in all this, as we told climate negotiators, they need to think of the local forest and learn that the issue of equity is not a luxury. It is a prerequisite.

In January 2001, Anil lost his long battle to cancer. I had already taken over the running of CSE a few years ago as his health had deteriorated. But the task ahead was formidable. How would I sustain the high-quality work of the organisation without him? It seemed impossible.

But what I learnt quickly enough was to draw upon the ideas, perspectives and courage that he had instilled in me. My task was also easier because colleagues who had worked with Anil and were steeped in his values stayed on at the organisation. Most importantly, my mother was there for support and guidance.

We pushed and prodded for change. Our campaign for the right to clean air reached a peak in 2002, as our demand for transition to Compressed Natural Gas (CNG) was accepted. All public transport buses and three-wheelers in the capital city moved to CNG, which brought down pollution. People in Delhi could see the stars again. Health indicators improved. Now we are seeking second-generation reforms, so that the city invests in public transport, walking and cycling. This will be our tryst with environment and health security.

right
A woman farmer from West Bengal crossing a green paddy field. Women play a crucial role in every dimension of agriculture and work shoulder to shoulder with men.

Similarly, work on community-based water management strategies in rural India, and for a new paradigm for sewage management in urban India has taken shape, captured policy space and is now moving to practice.

I believe India has a huge challenge to reinvent the way in which it will manage growth, so that in the future, it is both inclusive and sustainable. Women have a special role in that since we know that women and environment have a special relationship. It is they who have the responsibility to care for basic needs of the family—water or firewood. For instance, they are the ones who collect water for drinking and as water gets scarce or gets polluted, they have to walk longer and longer distances. They understand the pain of degradation; they are the first to argue that environment must be protected and regenerated at any cost. Apart from the Chipko movement, women in many other villages have worked tirelessly to plant trees or restore traditional water bodies. Their leadership in this area has provided the country the direction it needs to manage its resources and to look for the critical balance between environment and development.

We cannot afford the high-cost way of the already industrialised world, to clean up our environment. These countries had the money to invest in cleaning and they did. But because they never looked for big solutions, they always stayed behind the problem—local air pollution is still a problem in most Western cities, even if the air is not as black as ours. It is just that the toxin is smaller, more difficult to find or to smell.

In India and other developing countries, the temptation is to emulate the already rich, and their environment-unfriendly ways, with much lesser resources and much more inequity and poverty. The fact is, we cannot find answers in the same half solutions they invested in. This is our challenge. We can do things differently to reinvent growth without pollution. But only if we have the courage to think differently. I hope we will.

left
A wind farm installed at Badabagh, Rajasthan—a historically significant garden fort which was built nearly 300 years ago by Jai Singh II. It has four turbines and produces 12 GWh (Gigawatt hours) electricity annually. To fulfil the rapidly increasing energy requirements of the country, India is turning towards environment-friendly ways to generate electricity.

Invest upon Learning

Naina Lal Kidwai

A few months ago, I heard from Gauriben, who lives in a small village in Gujarat. Today, she is the leader of a team of women in her village who relentlessly worked towards attaining water-security in their homes through rain-water harvesting and other innovative methods. I first met her at a SEWA (Self Employed Women's Association, an internationally renowned NGO with 1.7 million women members) meeting in Gujarat, where she stood up and simply said, 'My name is Gauriben'. When I asked why that was important, she told me that five years ago, she was known just as the mother of her son or the wife of her husband. But today, she is Gauriben—a newly earned identity for herself in her family and society that respects her for her contribution to bettering life in her village, with the help of SEWA, which opened up livelihood opportunities for many like her. It gladdens me to realise that my life and profession has taken me all the way from Harvard to rural India, and that is where my heart lies. Like Gauriben, every woman has a mission and an intriguing story that defines her identity. Reliving the memories and experiences of my life that have made me the woman I am today, is a reminder that everything is possible with the right opportunities and determination and, of course, some luck.

Born into a conventional North Indian family, I spent the first ten years of my life at my home in Mumbai where my sister and I learnt the first lessons of our lives from our parents. My father headed an insurance company. I recollect instances of him organising business meetings at home, and at times, my going in the car to his office as late as nine o' clock at night to bring him back home. I simply loved the look and feel of his office, and that leather swivel chair on which he sat, which never failed to capture the imagination of the little girl in me. As unbelievable as it may sound, I think I almost knew that was where I wanted to be—the corporate world.

At eleven, I joined Tarahall, Loreto Convent's boarding school at Simla. The school was run by Catholic nuns, who took pains to strengthen the moral fibre in us, which we imbibed unconsciously. It was a great decision by my parents to send me to a school where invaluable traits of leadership, team spirit, and qualities such as integrity and morality were imparted, all of which have stayed with me ever since.

The city of mountains and snow appealed to me instantaneously. However, there were some challenges—the school curriculum, which included Hindi as a main language (whereas I had studied Marathi till then), and participation in team games, of which I had no experience. Getting good marks in Hindi was crucial in attaining good overall grades. That was the first challenge in my life. So, I pushed myself, put in that extra effort and made sure that I mastered the new subject. Then, to obtain a position of leadership in the new environment, I also had to demonstrate my skills on the playing field. From being a girl who didn't know the basics of basketball or ever playing in a team, I went on to being in the school basketball and badminton teams that eventually won the state championships. These were my initial lessons in leadership and adaptability, where I had to constantly adapt myself and acquire new skills and knowledge as each situation demanded.

I remember the discussion I had with my father regarding my higher education, and we decided to tread an unchartered path. I chose to pursue a graduate course in economics and then follow it up with chartered accountancy. I was a science stream student till Class XII, and economics was a new subject for me. But I had a clear goal, which was to enter the corporate world, possibly in the banking sector. In those days, India did not have many women in senior positions for me to emulate, so we were unsure how these plans would evolve.

I was fortunate to be able to join one of India's leading institutions, Lady Shri Ram College (LSR) in Delhi University to get my BA (Honours) in Economics. I soon found myself engaged in a multitude of activities in the college, from debates to dramatics, from student union activities to art festivals, from academics to elections. Fond memories of the debates and competitions where one stretched one's limits to win, fun memories of delivering speeches standing on coffee tables at the college canteen for election campaigning, exhilarating memories of being elected as the secretary and then president of the student's union, quirky memories of the college principal pointing out that I was the first president in trousers and not in the traditional

left
Naina Lal Kidwai, during an interview in Mumbai. She has been ranked several times in the Fortune global list of Top Women in Business, in the Wall Street Journal and Financial Times Global Listing of Women to Watch and also been listed by *Time* magazine as one of their 15 Global Influential Persons 2002.

salwar kameez. But the most gratifying moment of them all, was conducting the first LSR college festival—Tarang, for which I had to be very persuasive to convince the principal to let boys from other colleges enter our campus and participate in the festival; an annual festival that LSR is proud of, even today.

I had ample opportunities to hone my leadership skills in college, thanks to the broad spectrum of extra-curricular activities that we participated in. Even today, when I recruit young professionals, I look out for their exposure and participation in such activities, as I believe that it makes them well-rounded personalities. The Indian education sector needs to lay more emphasis on the overall personality development of our students, rather than focusing on just achieving a degree.

Soon after college, I joined Price Waterhouse as an articled clerk in 1977 after urging them to consider hiring women—there were three of us as their first women employees. I applied to the Harvard Business School and became the first Indian woman to graduate from there. I discovered that post-boxes in America were blue in colour and not red; I also learnt that 'drug stores' in America sell ice-cream. So much for the uninitiated twenty-three-year-old who had travelled out of the country for the first time, and was the youngest student in the class. But I have to confess that I was well armed in coping abilities and adaptability, when compared to many of my classmates. My knowledge of the English language was sound, so was my capacity to multi-task and learn new things every day. I do believe that Indian education equips you to withstand stress and perform under duress.

On graduation from Harvard, I had several offers to work in the US, but I had made up my mind to return to India. I tell many young graduates that if you want to make a difference, India is the place that provides that opportunity. It is often better to be a big fish in a small pond rather than a minnow in a vast ocean. I am glad with my decision to return, as I have been able to contribute to the growth of the Indian economy in my small way, participating in decisions to set up the National Stock Exchange, the National Stock Depository, the rules regarding insider trading, various governance issues and working on India's first privatisations. On my return to India, I worked with Grindlay's Bank and then moved on to Morgan Stanley. I have been with HSBC since 2002.

The year 2013 was an interesting year as the first woman president of Federation of Indian Chambers of Commerce and Industry (FICCI), India's oldest apex chamber of commerce and industry. Juggling my work at HSBC and FICCI wasn't easy, but the learning was well worth it, especially because of the deep insights into various industries and the interactions with large trade delegations led by prime ministers and presidents of countries like the UK, France, Kuwait, China etc. I had an opportunity to push the cause of safety for women at the workplace and to form the Inclusive Governance Council to provide a meeting point for the industry with regulators, policy makers and civil society, while we look for constructive ways to improve governance in India. I believe that it is worthwhile for those inclined to join an area of interest in FICCI, to impact thinking in that sector. I have chaired the Capital Markets and Financial Inclusion Committees and started the Water Mission at FICCI—experiences which were gratifying, as I believe I could contribute and learn.

right
Women are believed to be gifted with a natural financial aptitude. Indian women play a significant role in the nation's economy not just by contributing productively to it, but also with their acumen for saving and frugality.

Fixed Deposit Rates

PERIOD	INT % p.a	YIELD % p
15 DAYS TO 29 DAYS	03.25	
30 DAYS TO 59 DAYS	3.25	
60 DAYS TO 89 DAYS	3.60	
90 DAYS TO 17▮	3.60	
180 DAYS	3.75	
270 DAY▮	3.75	
12 MTH▮	4.00	
18 MTH▮	4.00	
> 25 MTH▮	4.25	
> 36 MTHS T▮	4.25	4
> 41 MTHS T▮	4.50	4

My philosophy in life is of continuous learning. I consider myself an intellectual sponge...absorbing knowledge wherever possible. Learning today has moved away from rote and more towards analysis, which is crucial in distilling the knowledge gained. Some of the biggest turning points in my life have been learning from failures. Picking oneself up, not getting disheartened and analysing the reasons for the mistakes. It is important to stretch oneself, to move out of one's comfort zone and, therefore, keep evolving.

Whenever I meet young entrepreneurs or students, I get asked about the challenges that I faced as a woman banker. I think that in the initial stages, every career woman faces some discrimination, lack of acceptance, work-life balance and other such challenges. However, you quickly reach a point in your career when people focus on your contributions, irrespective of your gender. Ultimately, it has really got to do with your professional capability, the reputation you build in the field and being a good team player. Especially in the corporate world, I think it is easier for a woman in India to progress in her career than in a number of Western countries. Companies in the West will often have a culture of visiting pubs on Thursdays and golfing on weekends. An Indian company is quite diverse, with people of different habits, where no one needs to conform to any stereotyped pattern. It makes it easier for women to belong to a diverse group where social expectations are not as demanding. However, women do need to network more to progress. We are fortunate to have the advantage of extended families and affordable domestic help to enable us to attend to our careers.

It is important to have an understanding spouse and family support. My husband Rashid Kidwai has been doing some amazing work with SEWA, transforming lives of many in rural India. I hope to continue to work towards creating livelihood and economic opportunities for underprivileged women and have been fortunate to be engaged in the work of Grassroots Trading Network for Women and assisting my husband in his efforts to improve the lives of underprivileged women.

I look forward to family vacations with our son and daughter in wild life parks and mountains. We enjoy bird watching, and just being in the forest with the rich flora and fauna, instead of only being on a perennial hunt for sighting the tiger. Sometimes one just needs to stay put in the middle of a deep, dark forest; to savour the stillness, to seek some calm and to remind oneself that *the woods are lovely dark and deep, but I have promises to keep and miles to go before I sleep*.

right (top)
An employee working at a Mumbai branch of HSBC bank. The last few years have seen rising confidence in the leadership capabilities of women, and a strengthening of their role in the Indian banking sector. Among fifty-two CEOs from the banking and financial sectors covered in a recent survey, fifteen were women.

right (bottom)
Inauguration of first branch of Bharatiya Mahila Bank in Delhi on 19 November 2013. BMB is India's first all-women bank created exclusively to cater to the needs of women. Increasing number of women CEOs in banking companies has seen a multiplier effect across the board as more women are joining the banking sector.

Life is Fair

Fathima Beevi

As I sip a hot cup of tea, sitting in my quaint abode nestled in the plush environs of the smallest district of Kerala, named Pathanamthitta—the first to have achieved the status of zero population growth in the country—I thank God for the eventful, fulfilling life that He has given me. I could not have asked for more, what with the myriad opportunities that life presented me with, to make a difference in the lives of many, to touch their lives with fair hands that dispensed justice. I often narrate to my grand-nieces and grand-nephews, the stories and experiences that have harmonised this eighty-seven-year-old woman's life. How did their grand-aunt become India's first female judge of the highest court of the land, they often ponder. To summarise the long story, I tell them, 'My father had a dream for me; and I simply lived his dream.'

Born as the eldest daughter to Meera Sahib and Khadeeja Beevi in 1927, I had five sisters and two brothers to fill my childhood with moments of delight and innocent joys that flood my memories even now. My father was a dreamer, who had very ambitious dreams for me. He ensured that all of us received good education and inspired us to make a career for ourselves; not just any career—but one that would provide relief to those in need, one that would be rooted in compassion and justice. I completed my schooling from the Catholicate High School, Pathanamthitta, and went on to do my Bachelors in Chemistry at University College, Trivandrum. In 1947, as soon as I graduated with a first division in BSc Chemistry, I enrolled for the much coveted Master's course in chemistry in the same university, partly because I did not want to veer away from the obvious path that lay in front of me—joining the academia—which was considered to be a highly suitable job for women in those days. But my father, who was a sub-registrar then, was adamant that I join Trivandrum Law College to pursue a Bachelor's degree in Law, because he felt that becoming a lawyer would enable me to serve the masses directly and create an impact on the lives of people by facilitating justice for them in all honesty and fairness. As naïve as a twenty-year-old could get, I left no stone unturned to cajole my father into accepting my decision to confine myself to learning and teaching chemistry. It was his firm importunity then that opened several doors of opportunities for me in what would be my passion for a life-time. I still wonder what would have given him that deep a level of insight and grit to encourage his six daughters to chase education and hold their heads high in a nation that seemed shaky and raw with the bruises of Partition, when Muslim girls educating themselves beyond a point was an instance of rarity.

I joined the Trivandrum Law College for my Bachelor's in Law. My real test of Islam awaited me there, when I was asked by the college authorities to speak on Prophet Mohammed to a boisterous, male-dominated audience—mostly peers, in dissonance with the decision to make a student, that too, a female student speak on such a sensitive issue as religion. After a lot of persuasion, they relented and I was allowed to speak, though I don't think I was a riveting orator then. College life was rife with such instances of subtle struggles and acts of cutting across planes of gender, religion and other societal barriers. To my defence, as a law student, I had always been confident of my abilities and such obstacles hardly deterred me. I was glad to see that during my term in college itself, there was a perceptible change in the mindset of my peers towards Muslim girls, as was seen in their welcoming Ayesha Beevi rather effusively, when she joined the course, braving all odds.

If you ask me to recollect the most memorable day of my life, I would emphatically say, 'The day I was enrolled into the Bar Council of India.' It was 14 November 1950; the day when the whole of India celebrated Pandit Jawaharlal Nehru's birthday in the year that India became a Republic, the day when a modest Muslim girl from South India was declared the topper of the Bar Council of India's exam, the first female lawyer to have ever accomplished that honour. My joy knew no bounds, but alas, I had a spin of mind and decided against actively practicing law at that point of time, probably because I instinctively knew that it would rake up another furore, and a very serious one it would be. Eventually, I did break the mould, and started practicing under CP Parameshwaran Pillai in Kollam district and stayed on there for eight years. Once I had established myself as a just and able lawyer, eager to deliver, I started gaining acceptance within the judicial circles and society at large.

left
Fathima Beevi has also served as the Chancellor of Madras University and the Chairman of Kerala Commission for Backward Classes. She was a member of National Human Rights Commission.

In 1958, I was appointed as Munsiff in the Kerala Sub-ordinate Judicial Services, elevated as the Sub-ordinate Judge in 1968 and was promoted as the Chief Judicial Magistrate in 1972. With the elevation to the High Court as a judge in 1983, I had reached a stage in my life where I had begun to feel that I was indeed living my father's dream; that I could offer solace to many a disconcerted soul, by waving the wand of justice. I had been exposed to innumerable facets of suffering, especially of women, in those days, when there was a surfeit of dowry-related cases and violence against women. I distinctly remember the minutest details of every case that came to me, and the duel that would ensue between the woman in me and judge in me, when I proclaimed the decision. As a woman, my heart always empathised with the victimised woman, but as a judge I had to decouple emotions from the sense of fairness, and the latter prevailed, without fail.

I retired as Judge of the High Court in 1989. I was soon appointed to the Supreme Court of India as its first ever female judge. I wouldn't deny the fact that it was challenging, but I can vouch for the absence of discrimination solely based on gender, whatsoever. I still vividly remember every morning of my tenure at the apex court, when all the judges would present themselves before the Chief Justice in his chamber who would allocate us the respective benches. When I retired from the apex court in April 1992, I had never imagined that life after retirement would be so intriguing. I was appointed as the first woman member of the National Human Rights Commission, an assignment that I cherish till date. My work then enabled me to travel the length and breadth of the country, bearing direct witness to the shackles that bound the people of my country. I also had the fortune to deliver gubernatorial duties between 1997 and 2001 when I was appointed Governor to the state of Tamil Nadu, which was not in one of its most politically stable phases then. Though I had to counter partisan forces of vested interests and stand the test of fire which lent me mute to the volley of questions that were hurled at me on submitting my resignation, it only reinstated my understanding that great power comes with great responsibilities. Greater your goal, greater the risk and greater the glory, I always remind the young minds effervescent with energy and ambitions.

right (top)
A woman praying outside a mausoleum in Nizamuddin Dargah, Delhi. Indian women draw strength from the virtues of their respective religions.

right (bottom)
Law graduates at the first convocation of National Law University, Delhi, a recently instituted world-class law university in the country. The President of India, Pranab Mukherjee, in his convocation speech urged the graduates to take up legal aid for the poor as a lifelong commitment and do their best to draw attention to the problems of the disempowered. 'Do it as your duty–your contribution to a more equal world and a motherland you are proud of, an India which has made you what you are today,' he said.

Islam as a religion has always stood me in good stead in my personal as well as social life. I have never worn a hijab in my life, but I always veil my head with the *pallu* of my sari. Talking of saris, I have to admit that I am very fond of sari shopping; right from a young age as a college girl, I have had an affinity towards white saris, and it stays on even now. I mostly prefer wearing white and off-white Kancheevaram silk saris with a coloured zari border. As much as I respect the art of cooking, I have to confess that I have never cooked, as my mother or my sister would always come to my assistance. As a fruit ripens and attains the zenith of sweet warmth, so does a human being in old age; many who can't resist their curiosity often ask me, 'Don't you now feel that life would have been better had you married?' To that I say, 'Life is always fair and beautiful.'

—as told to Divya S Iyer, Cynthia Chandran

Sky is Not the Limit

Padma Bandopadhyay

The sky in the Arctic used to feel so low…as if you could pluck the stars and the moon. After attending to patients in a nearby hospital, as I walked back to the residential station, I also had the luck of watching the beautiful aurora borealis. Wondering what fascinating work took me all the way to the Arctic Circle? At that point of time in my long journey, I was living in the North Pole for four months as part of an Indo-Russian physiology experiment, to determine if people from tropical climates and countries could acclimatise themselves to the extreme cold conditions.

November 1989 to February 1990 may have been the coldest time of the season, but I was used to the cold. As a forty-five-year-old Wing Commander, I had been posted at the Defence Institute of Physiology & Allied Sciences and had lived in the western and the eastern Himalayas in high altitude areas, researching acclimatisation methodologies for Indian soldiers and how they could avoid being affected by High Altitude Pulmonary Oedema and High Altitude Cerebral Oedema, HAPO and HACO in a mountaineer's language. I was, thus, selected to conduct research in the icy Arctic winter. The aim of this study was also to find out whether Indian soldiers coming from tropical climate would be able to perform their duties at their best. If yes, how long would the acclimatisation take and how long will the body's adjustment process last, once they leave the Arctic.

Forget the science, it was a Herculean task to convey our ideas to the then Soviets, with their poor English. It was terribly cold; the normal temperature was around -35 degree Celsius and further reduced by chilly winds, reaching up to -45 degree Celsius at times. We had ten Indian soldiers drawn from all parts of the country as subjects, and to compare, we also had thirty Russian soldiers in the study team. There was no electricity. Most of the scientific equipment operated on diesel and we worked round the clock. Many a times, the equipment would stop working and then we had to wait for it to be considerate to us and use whatever technology we knew! Most of the time, we tried our hands at repair and, lo and behold—it used to work.

On my return to India, I was awarded the Priyadarshini Award. I was the first woman then, to be awarded this medal. Later came greater recognition, membership of the Indian Society of Aerospace Medicines, the International Medical Society and the New York Academy of Sciences. On 26 June 2000, I was made the first woman Air Commodore of the Indian Air Force. I took over the command of the most prestigious Air Force Medical Unit, the Air Force Central Medical Establishment and was awarded Ati Vishisth Seva Medal for service of meritorious order on 26 January 2002. I became an Air Marshal in 2004.

You may wonder how a little girl from Tirupati, Padmavathy, daughter of Alamelu and V Swaminathan, a pious south Indian couple rooted deeply in values, ethics, customs and *samskaras* (rituals and traditions) became Air Marshal Padma Bandopadhyay, the first woman Air Marshal in the world. My family came to live in Delhi soon after Independence. When I was about five years old, we lived near Connaught Place. Right opposite our house on the main road was Dr S Padmavathy's bungalow. She was Professor of Medicine at Lady Hardinge Medical College then. My father read out her name and I was her namesake. Since that day, I had dreamt of becoming a doctor. I had not joined school then and I did not have the slightest idea how one became a doctor. There was no doctor in the family.

My mother suffered from Tuberculosis (TB) of the spine. At that time, many people suffered from TB, many due to lack of awareness and also of medical facilities. My mother was bedridden and immobile for about a decade. She was a young woman then and you can imagine her plight, not being able to look after herself, and more importantly, not being able to look after her children. She survived on just rice and curd at the Safdarjung Hospital in Delhi for a decade! I learnt from my mother the grit, tenacity and sheer will to survive under most adverse situations.

My father was young. He could have married again due to my mother's prolonged illness, as was the practice those days. But he stood firm like a rock and sold whatever property he had, to import medicines for my mother. He took upon himself

left
Padma Bandopadhyay commanded the Air Force Medical Services. She created history by becoming the first woman Air Marshall in the world, a post which is just one rank below the Chief of Air Staff.

the arduous task of bringing up three children single-handedly. My father taught us to work hard, to live within one's means (however frugal it was), to believe in God and self and most importantly, to be a good, honest and humane being.

After passing the Higher Secondary examination (then a three-year course) in the Arts group, I found myself topping the Board to the surprise of one and all, including myself.

I had seen my mother suffering at close quarters. I had become fond of the 'hospital smell', the dress of the 'care and cure' staff and their dedication towards patients. When I told my father that I wanted to write the pre-medical test, much against the advice of all relatives, he approached each and every college at Delhi University and requested the authorities to admit me in a 'pre-medical' course. People laughed at him, but he did not give up. With his perseverance, faith in his daughter's capability and God's blessings, I was finally admitted to the Kirori Mal College. History was made in Delhi University as I changed from the 'Arts' stream to the 'Science' stream. Later, I qualified for the prestigious Armed Forces Medical College to become a doctor.

During my pre-medical study days, the Indo-China war of 1962 broke out. Some of my childhood friends became martyrs in the severe climatic conditions in which the war was fought. The soldiers were neither acclimatised nor trained to face the operation scenario. The touching song by Lata Mangeshkar, *Mere watan ke logo,* brings tears to my eyes even today. That day, I decided to join the Armed Forces in any capacity and fight for my country.

bottom
Padma Bandopadhyay operating a recompression chamber at Institute of Aerospace Medicine at Bengaluru. The institute pioneered in establishing Hyperbaric Oxygen Therapy—a procedure performed to increase the oxygen content in blood—in India, in the year 1964.

right
Padma Bandopadhyay laying wreath at 'Amar Jawan Jyoti' at India Gate. Amar Jawan Jyoti is a memorial site which was added under the arch of India Gate and the flame burns continuously, day and night, in remembrance of the soldiers who sacrificed their lives to protect the nation in the Indo-Pakistan War of 1971.

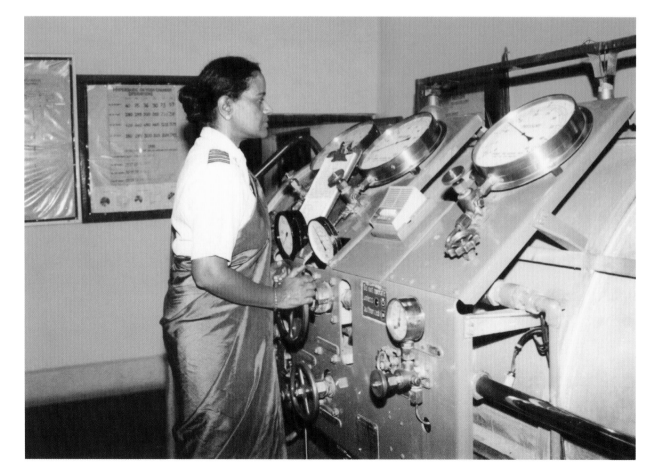

I found the Air Force uniform very impressive, aircraft flying adventurous and aerobatic manoeuvres breath-taking. Speed thrills, especially when one is young. I dreamt of becoming a pilot. It was only much later that I realised that not everyone in the Air Force is a pilot. The next best bet was to become an Aviation specialist, so that I could fly all the fast and furious aircrafts as a squadron Medical Officer. I was the first Aviation medical specialist in South East Asia. I flew in most of the fighter aircrafts of that time where I was posted, and this experience helped in understanding and mitigating many of the aero-medical issues.

The Air Force also gave me my life partner at Bengaluru, Prof Satinath Bandopadhyay, VSM, PhD from IIT, Delhi, and then a flight lieutenant. We fell in love and against all objections from friends and family members, got married in 1969. After Bengaluru, I was posted as the medical officer to the Air Force station at Halwara—a forward base very close to the Indo-Pak border. Here, I tried to set up an antenatal clinic and a family ward. I also improvised incubators for premature babies, which not only saved the lives of three babies but also brought laurels from superiors and families. My family too grew, at the same time. My loving husband supported me at each turning point of my life. During the 1971 war, my husband and I were posted at the western theatre. This experience taught me a lot to dare and do—camaraderie, human values and courage. It was a non-family station and we operated from bunkers at one point—medical wing, Base Ops or ATC etc. Our responsibility was to take care of all the Armed Forces' casualties from all over the western front, as we were the first field hospital in the chain of evacuation. Wounded soldiers with severe war injuries, mostly orthopaedic were brought in. We treated the wounds, stabilised

page 37
Indian Air Force cadets march during the passing out ceremony from Air Force Academy in Dundigal, near Hyderabad. An increasing number of women cadets are being inducted into the IAF each year; in 2013, a total of 200 student graduated from the Academy, out of which thirty-seven were women.

page 38
Indian Air Force pilots of the Surya Kiran Aerobatic Team (SKAT) display their skills during an air show, part of the platinum jubilee celebrations of the Indian Air Force at the Adampur Air Force Station, Punjab. The prestigious SKAT which was formed to serve as the "Ambassadors of the Indian Air Force" saw a woman officer in Flt Lt Bhavana Mehra as a co-pilot of Surya Kiran aircrafts. She was also a commentator on their manoeuvres.

the fractures and even carried out amputation as a life saving measure throughout the war.

The civilian population in the area, especially the women, contributed to the war efforts more than known to the outside world. During the day, they made delicious sweets for us and even knit beautiful sweaters for us. At night, they kept strict vigil in the adjoining wheat fields, captured almost all the enemy paratroopers who swooped down on our territory, gave them a nice welcome thrashing and handed them over to our security personnel. I still admire their courage, valour and patriotism. Real kudos to these unsung heroines! Following this Indo-Pak war, my husband and I were awarded the Vishishta Seva Medal together, at the same investiture ceremony, which is also a first in the armed forces of the world.

Many a times, women wonder whether they will have a raw deal, especially in the so-called 'male' bastion. Will they be able to break the glass ceiling? To become one amongst them, you should become one of them, and understand the issues faced in the work situation, especially in a 'real ops' scenario. Today, the times are far better than when we joined. In the Armed Forces, we get respect and freedom to do the job assigned. We should face challenges squarely and prove that we are equal partners.

As one lamp lights another, each successful woman must help others who are not so fortunate. Let us all share what God has bestowed on us. Never give up, try and try again and do not stop till you reach your goal, *Prayatnam Videheya, Prayatnam Videheya*. Jai Hind.

The Eternal Notes

Lata Mangeshkar

As Indian cinema celebrates hundred years of mesmerising the world and looks back at the eventful journey, I too feel blessed. I have had the rare honour of devoting seventy-one years of my life to this great industry—an industry which has given shape to a million dreams; an industry which has been spreading the fragrance of Indian culture the world over. And the industry that helped me earn the love and respect of millions.

Baba, my father, Deenanath Mangeshkar, was a great classical singer and I grew up breathing the air that swayed to musical notes and ragas. I was an intent listener and could remember every note even as a five-year-old, but could not muster enough courage to sing in his presence. And then one day, the transformation happened. Baba was teaching Raag Puriya Dhanashri to one of his students. As he moved out for some work, the young boy was practising the raga by himself. As always, though

I was playing, my ears were glued to the music. I felt the boy had gone off scale, and I couldn't stop myself from going up to him and singing the notes to show him the correct scale. That very moment Baba returned and heard me sing—for the first time! He immediately called my mother, Mai, as we called her, and announced, 'We have a good singer at home but never knew it.' Early morning the next day, Baba woke me up, and so began my learning under my guru—my father—with the same raga, Puriya Dhanashri.

My father owned a theatre company called Balwant Sangeet Mandali. He was a stage-actor and producer of musical plays, and considered a leading light of Marathi theatre. As a child, I was proud of being his daughter—daughter of such an eminent father—I still am today. We lived in reasonable affluence in a large house in Sangli, a small trading town in Maharashtra. I had a normal joyful childhood—a naughty and fun-loving child who had to be coaxed, at times, to learn music. All that started changing as Baba suffered huge losses in his newly-formed film company. We managed to run the house with the money that came from Baba's own concerts. We moved to Poona in 1940. Things turned from bad to worse as Baba's health started failing. And then on 24 April 1942 at 11:20 am, just at the moment he had himself predicted, I lost my Baba—my guru, to the hands of fate.

I was thirteen then, the eldest in the family, with three sisters—Meena, Asha and Usha, and brother Hridaynath. The responsibility of the family fell on my young shoulders. In the early 1940s, playback singing hadn't caught on, so acting became the only option. I managed to get a job in October 1942. And till 1947, I acted, first in Poona, then in Kolhapur and Bombay, even though I never liked it—the make-up, the hot lights, the endless takes and the chaos around. So much so, that the day I started working as a playback singer, I prayed to God to never make me act again. He listened! But before that, I had another crisis to overcome. Master Vinayak, the famous actor-director of his times, and in whose films I acted in minor roles, died in 1947. It was a big shock. His company had to be closed, so far my only source of income had been working with him. We used to live in a small official accommodation. All the nine of us—my immediate family members and my cousin Indira and her two children used to sleep in one small bedroom, but even that was on the verge of being taken away. It was as if life was back to square one—just like in 1942.

A new period of struggle began. Only this time, it also meant a new beginning. I started getting singing assignments. And thus began a bittersweet period of struggle and success, endless hours of work and the joys of working with wonderful people. Running from one studio to another; recording songs from morning till night; it never occurred to me that I could do anything else. There was just one preoccupying thought—that I must take care of my family and provide them with comfort, somehow. I feel grateful that I had to face great struggles, because only after great struggles does a human become human, otherwise you become arrogant. I faced so many struggles that my heart became peaceful.

A learned person once said, 'In your journey of life, consider every beast and man like a guru. You can learn something from everyone you come across.' I believe in that as well. As the bee gathers honey, so you gather lessons from every situation.

left
Lata Mangeshkar during the Inaugural MTV IMMIES in Mumbai, where she received an Inspiration award. She has recorded around 30,000 songs from 1948 to 1987 and is listed in *Guinness Book of World Records* for recording highest number of songs between 1974 and 1991.

Ghulam Haider Sahib, singing for whom was my first big break, advised me to ensure that I sing each word clearly. It is only because of the blessings of such gurus and the kindness of God that I have sung in thirty-six languages without being formally educated in even one. I learnt Marathi at home and picked up Hindi, Urdu and Sanskrit only after growing up, so as to ensure that I respect the power of words.

I have seen a lot in life, yet I don't regret the past and for the future, I want to ensure that I help people. Together as a family, we started the Deenanath Mangeshkar Hospital & Research Centre in Pune. Here, we provide free medicare for orphaned children. We also set up a cancer research centre. Deenanath Mangeshkar Kala Mandir hosts theatre and musical events in Goa, near my ancestral village. I strongly believe people should live in harmony with each other and spread joy and peace.

Nobody should ever think that he or she has achieved everything in life, especially because music is something in which you can never achieve perfection. Howsoever deep you may go, deeper is this ocean. I do realise that change is inevitable with the passage of time. Our lifestyle, the cities, the environment, the economy…everything has changed; and so has music. But I would urge the youth of our nation to put in their heart and soul into keeping the tradition and reverence for art alive. Those interested in music should pay more attention to Indian classical music. I have sung many film songs as also songs with a classical base—but I really wanted to sing classical music. That remains an unfulfilled desire for me. I hope the younger singers, especially women, will have more worthy opportunities to prove their mettle. In today's world of technology, when life tends to get mechanised, I hope they don't get lost in the maze, but help build the bridge between culture and convenience. That is my only prayer for the much smarter and talented younger generation.

My greatest gift is music—it is my life, my God. How else would you feel when you are estimated to have sung 30,000 songs? When a nation of a billion people not only bestows on you its highest civilian honour, the Bharat Ratna, but also gives you the greatest blessing you can receive—its love? If I am gifted, it is by the grace of God. If I were to live a thousand years, I would not be able to repay the gratitude. That is why I pray to God that if I am to be born again, may I be born again as an Indian and in Maharashtra…

—with Shobit Arya

right
Lata Mangeshkar during a performance. She always sings barefoot as a mark of respect to the platform where she sings. Referred to as Nightingale of India, Lata has attended school for just one day in her life, but has been awarded honorary doctorates from six universities around the world.

Tryst with Economics

Gita Gopinath

As I walk up the stairs of Harvard's economics department to my office, I frequently glance at the portraits that line the stairwell—of the past Harvard economists who altered the course of economic thinking—all men. At such moments, I feel a sense of pride, humility and disbelief, all at the same time. It is fair to say that attaining tenure at Harvard's economics department exceeded even my wildest dreams as a girl studying in the small town of Mysore. It is made even sweeter that I happen to be just the fourth woman and the first Asian woman to be tenured in the history of this department. When I reach my office, I stare at the name board of my colleague Amartya Sen, whose office is adjacent to mine. To be next door to Amartya, whose lecture at the Delhi School of Economics in 1993 inspired my journey into academia is such a high!

I come from a fairly conventional South Indian family, with both my parents—TV Gopinath and VC Vijayalakshmi—hailing from the state of Kerala. But I spent my formative years in Mysore, a small and beautiful town where I did most of my schooling. Growing up in Mysore, I wasn't exactly exposed to career-oriented and ambitious women role models. Fortunately, my parents, especially my father, nurtured several dreams and had aspirations for his two daughters, which made having a role model quite unnecessary.

When I was in my early teens, my father was convinced that I should become the next PT Usha. I was a good runner and won my races, mostly because I tended to be taller than the others in my group. However, I hated it! What I loved most was learning. There is something magical about the moment when you truly comprehend something. So I wanted to spend all my days with my books. It took me a while to convince my father that he had some sort of a geek for a daughter, and not an athlete!

Now for how I ended up as an economist—that was accidental in so many ways. I was a student of science until pre-university and was quite good at it. It was, however, my father's dream that I join the Indian Administrative Service (IAS). My cousin Vinod made out the case to my parents that I needed to go to Delhi to study economics, as it is a winning subject for the IAS exams. So, I landed up in Delhi and appeared for the admission interviews for undergrad courses at the premier Lady Shri Ram College (LSR). Here, I first got interviewed for Political Science and did well enough for the admissions committee to tell me to enrol. At this point, I told them that I would also like to be interviewed for Economics before making a decision, as I preferred it to Political Science. This naïve response, not surprisingly, resulted in the committee full of political scientists, giving me a mouthful! With a heavy heart, I went up to the senior student who was listing students' names for various subjects. I told her my story. I had given up in less than a moment, and was ready to be enrolled for Political Science.

After understanding the situation, this senior simply told me that I did not have to make any decision under pressure and if Economics is what I wished to pursue, then that is what I should pursue! This person, unknown to me, is the reason I ended up studying economics at LSR. It was her strength of character that made her stand up for me—a random student from a small town—and made all the difference to my future. That one moment still remains clearly etched in my memory.

Delhi was overwhelming for me in more ways than one. I had moved from a not-so-famous school in Mysore to LSR, where many of my classmates were from well-known Delhi schools. They were very confident, had strong public speaking skills, tremendous extra-curricular experience and a global outlook, with several of them having travelled the world. Despite the differences, I was completely unapologetic about my small town background and refused to be intimidated by anyone. I still carry that attitude when I deal with new situations and surroundings. Even when I went to the US, and now, as I often find myself in new gatherings with Nobel laureates or high-level policy makers or other dignitaries, I remind myself that I am my own person, with a lot to contribute, and I deserve the same respect that everyone else in the room does.

LSR was a fantastic experience, as I discovered the exciting world of economics, participated in economic debates and analysed the 1991 economic crisis very closely.

left
Gita Gopinath, the celebrated economist, speaks on the potential of the Indian economy, at the World Economic Forum summit in Gurgaon. She was chosen as one of the Young Global Leaders by WEF in 2011.

When I was still in college, India was going through a serious economic crisis due to the large and growing fiscal imbalances of the 1980s. To study economics in the midst of this crisis was fascinating. It showed me how getting policies right could make an important difference to the health of economies and, therefore, to the lives of people. The intricacies of international trade and finance made only partial sense to me and I realised the need to further my education. The reason why I am an international economist today is largely because of these experiences back in college.

My bachelor's degree in economics in 1992 was followed by a first Master's at the Delhi School of Economics and a second in the US at University of Washington in 1996. When I decided to go to the US for further studies, I was sure of one thing—I didn't want to be a financial burden on my parents. So I went to the university that fully paid for my tuition and living expenses. Even though my parents were willing to bear certain expenses, I insisted on taking a loan to pay for my flight ticket and to buy clothes for myself.

After receiving my doctorate at Princeton, with fantastic advisers like Ken Rogoff, Ben Bernanke and Pierre-Olivier Gourinchas, I taught at the University of Chicago, at the Booth School of Business from 2001 to 2005, and then moved to Harvard, where I was first invited as a visiting Assistant Professor for a semester in 2005. At the end of that stint, the department made me an offer to stay. I was then granted tenure at Harvard's economics department in 2010. Tenure is sought-after amongst American university academia because it provides the guarantee of life-time appointment, and therefore, the freedom to pursue big and risky research ideas.

I am happy to be where I am today, and am fully aware that reaching here wasn't completely my own doing. It was an arduous journey, where several hands came forward to help me. My parents laid the foundation for my beliefs and value systems, emphasised on education and hard work. It is perhaps the matriarchal roots of my family that enabled me to grow up in an environment where a girl is considered very valuable. I had little reason for self-doubt and felt very worthy as a person. My sister Anita remains very protective and keeps me grounded. Growing up in Mysore also gave me some of my best friends—Veena, Priya and Bharat.

Life turned even more wonderful once I met my husband Iqbal Dhaliwal. Although I did not follow through on my father's dreams of joining the IAS, I did marry an IAS topper. Iqbal topped the Civil Services exam in 1996 and made my father a very happy person!

Iqbal is my rock. It is his unfaltering support that keeps me going through new challenges and professional upheavals. An economist himself, Iqbal is currently the Deputy Director of the Jameel Poverty Action Lab, at Massachusetts Institute of Technology. When I treat our ten-year-old son Rohil to a blast of economic constructs over dinner, I am often reminded of my mother's play school, which she runs upholding Gandhian values, with utmost sincerity and dedication towards every child who steps in, to be under her wings.

It is often said that women are deterred from entering the domain of economics and academia, due to a lack of role models. To ensure that more women receive tenure at top places, there needs to be a strong pipeline of women candidates, and once

they enter the academic profession, they must receive requisite mentoring. I believe women benefit from being mentored by other women. Networking and collaboration is an important part of any profession and when it is mainly male dominated, it can become harder for women to get ahead. There are not necessarily conscious forms of discrimination, but conscious effort has to be made to ensure women have a level playing field.

Having said that, we should not overlook the fact that women economists are now cracking the proverbial glass ceiling. More women economists count among the international economists viewed as global thought leaders. Some of my own research with co-authors led to the adoption of novel fiscal interventions by President François Hollande of France. At the end of the day, to have a successful career as a woman, one needs to constantly defy stereotypes, cultivate inner strength that pushes you forward and build a strong support system that makes the whole journey a lot more fun.

—as told to Anu Singh

Microfinance has played an important role in Indian women's empowerment. According to a study, 98 per cent of women who had used it for fiancial independence felt that it helped them in expression of opinions freely and in the role of decision-making in family.

Packing a Punch

MC Mary Kom

Strong, confident and unstoppable, Mary Kom is the picture of powerful will and determination, an idol India looks up to.

right
Mary Kom, the 'darling of Manipur' in a traditional attire consisting of Mekhala—a traditional wraparound skirt, and Innaphi—the shawl.

Born into a working-class family, as the eldest child to Mangte Tonga Kom and Mangte Akham Kom, my grandmother endearingly named me Chungneijang, which means 'prosperous' in the local dialect spoken by the Kom tribal community. My life's journey from the Jhum fields of Manipur to the boxing ring of London Olympics—the story of how Chungneijang transformed into Magnificent Mary, as they call me now—is no more a secret. I feel blessed and proud to be associated with the sport of boxing. I have seen it grow from its nascent stage to where it now stands—as a prime sport for youngsters in India.

All the widespread media attention sprung out of the miracle that surfaced in the form of the bronze medal at London Olympics in 2012. Even though I had bagged the world championship in boxing over five times between 2002 and 2010, it was difficult to even get adequate sponsors for my sporting needs and the extensive travelling that it necessitated. Today, my family's face has lit up in joy and the state of Manipur proudly celebrates my victory. They even have an anthem which goes *Mary Kom, Champion, Queen of the Ring*. And I stand humbled in front of the whole country, as I receive the prayers and encouragement of numerous people from every corner of India. Seeing the amount of happiness that my medal can bring on people's faces, I feel extremely content.

After narrating my life in my autobiography, *Unbreakable*, which was released in December 2013, I am now excited about the upcoming biopic, involving some of the best talents of the Indian film industry. When the filmmakers came to meet me, they were taken aback at my trim appearance. Despite being the mother of three wonderful boys—my five-year-old twins, and the young Prince who was born in 2013—I am as slender as a reed. I have chosen to take a break from sports in order to savour the bliss of motherhood in its entirety. That is the best thing that has ever happened to me—being a mother.

It's been a long journey with highs and lows in equal measure. Every moment in my life, every activity in my day, every person in my vicinity has played an important role in making me who I am today. As the elder sibling to two sisters and a brother, I used to lend a hand in household chores as well as physically demanding work in the fields. Very frequently, I had to carry my siblings in baskets tied to my back, as we climbed through the picturesque lands and hills of Manipur. It was good that we were poor, so we learnt to work really hard to earn a living. The tough upbringing helped me gain physical stamina, even as a young girl, which eventually dialled up my interest in sports and athletics in school. My father was an amateur wrestler and encouraged me to play in the village playground, at par with the boys my age. I was not very good at studies, and when my teachers are asked about Mary Kom today, they say, 'She was a wild sporty child racing up and down…' I was very keen on learning martial arts, and didn't know much about boxing in those days. I studied till high school in the village of Moirang, and later came to Imphal in order to take up sports in school.

I started athletics in 1999, with discus throw and shot put. I didn't even tell my family when I started boxing. In the year 2000, I was declared the best boxer at the state-level sub-junior boxing championship, which was my first match. A local newspaper carried my photo, which caught my father's attention. He got concerned about my future as a woman if I took to boxing. He was worried that it could ruin my looks and come in the way of my marriage and raising a family. But then he remembered how fast and strong I was, even as a child, and said, 'Maybe God has given her this gift for boxing.' That's when I started taking the game seriously.

My first boxing coach, Kosana Meitei, recently revealed on international television that he still remembered the diminutive young girl from a poor family, dressed in worn out track suits, hopping her way in and out of the boxing arena, full of grit and fired with passion for the game. Yes, it was a difficult climb, with several obstacles on the way to the medal. But I kept faith in God, which I believe came to my rescue every time my steps faltered. People, especially boys in my locality, would jeer at me and boo me, saying that boxing was meant for them, and I should not be trying my hand at it. I tried to explain to them to be mindful of their words and gestures, but never raised my hand against them even though I knew that my fist could strike a lightning blow.

When I started moving out of my state, Manipur, which was tucked away in an inconspicuous corner of the country, I realised that people from other parts of the country could not quite connect with me and some even discriminated against me. When I started going abroad for boxing championships, people would ask me if I belonged to China or Thailand or Japan, and simply not believe me when I said I was an Indian. These barriers and differences have disappeared now, and when I see the whole of my country and the world bestowing stardom and respect upon me, my heart swells with pride. India has credited me with the Arjuna Award, the Rajiv Gandhi Khel Ratna Award, the Padma Shri, the Padma Bhushan; and more importantly—the wholehearted support and acceptance of this woman from the North East. My heart is full of India; and my dream is to create a second Mary Kom, and a third, and many more.

To realise the larger goal of promoting boxing as a favoured sporting event for the generations to come, I started my boxing academy in Langol in the year 2004, close to my own residence, where I train thirty-seven young students in boxing. Sixteen of them are girls, and many of them stay there and look up to me not just as Madame Mary, but as their own mother. I train them in physical fitness and basic boxing moves, but the setup lacked adequate infrastructure, like a boxing ring, punching bag and boxing gear. Thanks to the award of ₹75 lakh announced by the Ministry of Sports in India soon after my Olympic win, I can now expand my academy and contribute to my country in a more wholesome way. I hope one day I will be to create an Olympic boxing champion from my students.

I myself plan to enrol into a three-month physical fitness training course in 2014 to warm up and get ready for the Rio 2016 Olympics, where I hope to bring back the Olympic Gold and live up to the expectations of my people. I had a technical difficulty in the 2012 Olympics where I had to punch in the 51kg category. I mostly used to participate in the 48kg category and had to gain weight without losing any of my stamina and power. The governing body of amateur boxing (AIBA) has been trying to introduce more weight categories for women in Rio in 2016, which, if it comes through, would raise my chances of winning the Gold that eluded me in London.

People have often asked me how it is to be a woman boxer in the male bastion. I think it is very important to realise and feel that you are a woman; and not pretend or even wish to be a man. That in itself instills self-confidence in a woman. I love the grace of womanhood when I wear Indian clothes, when I am at home taking care of my children and family. My victory in life and career is actually the story of how a man can be the pillar of support and guiding light in a woman's life. In the year 2000,

right
Mary Kom trains her students at her boxing academy in Manipur. Her achievements are a great inspiration to her students and she always encourages the young generation to chase their dreams and have faith in God.

I met my husband Onler, who was then the president of North East students' body in Delhi and had come forward to help me on hearing that my passport and bag had been stolen on a train from Manipur to Delhi. We courted for four years before walking down the aisle. Ever since I've known him, he has been my best friend, a keen observer of my game strategies, a great home maker and a wonderful father. The woman in me takes over when I step out of the boxing ring. As frivolous as it may sound, I often have my practice sessions with male boxers, as I find it difficult to punch pretty faces of women in the ring. Sometimes after a match, I feel very disturbed to see some injuries that I may have inflicted upon my opponent during the course of the game. There are several instances when I have walked up to the opponent, said sorry and wiped the blood off their noses.

Sasha's melodious number 'I am lonely, lolololonely...' keeps ringing aloud in my ears when I wait my turn on the turf; I feel that once I get into the ring, I am alone, all by myself. Not even the best of my coaches can help me then. Hence, at the Olympic match, even when my boxing coach Charles Atkinson, who had made a great difference to my training, was not allowed to accompany me, I was not perturbed. I felt secure in the hands of God. I pray to God before and after every session and every match, to make me unshakable and fearless in the game. As I step into the ring, I pray for about three seconds and always remember the story of David and Goliath in the Bible. I marvel at the wonder of David, a small boy whose victory over Goliath, a big man was due to God's power alone. I feel that I am also a small woman, hailing from a small state, and have to punch and conquer big rings on global platforms—only if God reveals His power through me.

right
Mary Kom trains at the Shri Shiv Chhatrapati Sports Complex, Balewadi in Pune, during a training session for the 2012 London Olympics. Boxer Dingko Singh's victory at the 1998 Asian Games inspired here immensely.

EVERY

WOMAN

IS

HER

Insights into some of the path-breaking
endeavours of Indian women.

A Million Smiles

Ela R Bhatt, social reformer

'Peace is not about lack of activities of war. It is not just about general elections. Peace is substantive, lasting; it is about life. It is about the ordinariness of life, how we understand each other, share meals, and share courtyards. And that is what women do. That very ordinariness as well as the kinds of livelihoods that so many women pursue is absolutely central to life. That is what keeps communities together,' says Ela Bhatt, who has changed the lives of close to twenty lakh women in rural India, through Self Employed Women's Association (SEWA) and several other organisations that she has set up.

Elaben (sister) is what she is endearingly known as in Gujarat, and in most of the world. Clad in a simple crisp handloom sari, her silver hair centrally parted and neatly tucked into a low bun and a stark bindi on her forehead, this eighty-four-year-old Gandhian's reassuring smile makes one instantly connect with her, as if she were family.

'Today, the lives of my family members hang on by the thread of my embroidery,' says Rambhaben, one of the thousands of craftswomen in Banaskantha district of western Gujarat, who have been assisted by SEWA to form a society and get fair price for their mirror-work products. The Lijjat papad tastes crispier when one knows there is SEWA's hand behind its rolling. From bee-keeping to computerised accounting, SEWA is the answer for millions of such women who seek to support themselves and their families.

SEWA was registered in 1972 as a trade union of self-employed women in Ahmedabad, following a cascade of unprecedented events. A lawyer by training, and a Gandhian by thoughts, Ela Bhatt, all of twenty-two then, was serving as the chief of the women's wing at Textile Labour Association. TLA is India's oldest and largest union of textile workers, founded in 1920 by Anasuya Sarabhai, who was inspired by the successful protest that Mahatma Gandhi had led in 1917 for the rights of textile workers. A group of migrant women labourers working at the Ahmedabad cloth market approached TLA, seeking redressal of their grievances. Ela, whose heart melted at the plight of these young women with no roof over their heads, wrote an article for the local newspaper, detailing the problems of women workers. The cloth merchants countered the charges with a news article of their own, denying the allegations and testifying to their fair treatment of the head-loader women. TLA women's wing turned the release of this story to its advantage by reprinting the merchant's claims on the cards and distributing them, to use as leverage with the merchants.

Soon, the word of this effective ploy spread and a group of used-garment dealers approached TLA's women's wing with their own grievances. A public meeting of used-garment dealers was called and over a hundred women attended. During the meeting in a public park, a woman from the crowd suggested they form an association of their own. Thus, on an appeal from the women and at the initiative of the leader of TLA's women's wing, Ela Bhatt, and its president, Arvind Buch, Self Employed Women's Association (SEWA) was born in December 1971.

They encountered challenges at every stage of growth—to establish it as a trade union since there was no precedent in the unorganised sector, to mobilise support and resources for effective functioning, to gain acceptance amongst the masses, to register the SEWA bank and its cooperatives, to not succumb under duress, to mitigate contingencies such as riots, earthquakes and political upheavals in Gujarat and finally the ties with TLA which had to be severed by 1981, owing to incompatibility of ideologies between the two organisations. Ever since, SEWA has grown faster and wider, leaving footprints of self-reliance and economic independence on the courtyards of many a hut in rural India.

Gandhi's statement, *'jan jan nu swaraj leva nu che'* (we have to achieve freedom for each and every individual) kept ringing in Ela's head all through her days of struggle, and served as a guiding light for her mission. 'I have not been alone in my endeavour. We failed many times, but it only made us more resilient. SEWA was the first formal body of workers in the informal sector across the world. As a strategy, the SEWA union worked with its cooperatives. If there were no crèches, then we built a crèche. When low wages was the issue, we earned the bargaining power

left
Ela Bhatt addresses a gathering of young women working in the informal sector in Ahmedabad. In 2013, she was awarded the Indira Gandhi prize for promoting peace as a 'tribute to her unflinching zeal towards the betterment of women in society'.

by understanding the world of work and where we stood, whether it was garment production or agriculture,' says Elaben.

Taking an innovative step, SEWA formed cooperatives cutting across sectors such as production, sales, marketing, social security, research, development, insurance, pension and housing and Elaben attributes her success to this wide arc of initiative.

'That brought self-reliance, which in turn brought bargaining power and then the capacity to enter the mainstream market. You have to be patient. I am not a person in a hurry. Always be goal-oriented. I know where to go and have a clear vision for the future, though there isn't a blue print. I would carefully listen to the members and live their lives in the field, with them. It's a two-way education. I learnt almost everything from the members of SEWA, their perspectives, their lives, their livelihoods. It's a sea of knowledge,' she explains. SEWA is recognised by several international bodies as one of the world's largest anti-poverty programmes. Through SEWA, Elaben has always emphasised on asset ownership in the name of women, raising productivity and capacity building for its members.

Half a century of work at the grassroots has presented her with a bouquet of memories. One that stands out is her field visit to the Machli Pith slums, which opened her eyes to a totally new world—the world of poverty and a lifetime of love from her would-be husband, who was leading her team then. 'Ramesh and I were classmates. He was very handsome. Being a student leader, an intellectual and an activist, he was selected to conduct pre-survey and pre-study before the first census of India. I was a part of his team in Surat, where we went to the Machli Pith slum. I didn't feel any disgust at what I saw, but this was a different world for me and I wasn't too easy in it. I admired him as I saw him mixing around freely, asking questions. He opened my eyes to this world. That influenced me deeply. I didn't understand poverty then. Much later, I got to understand it and am still learning. After marriage, he had to earn for the family and he taught at the university. He would often say, "You are doing what I wanted to do,"' she recollects.

Some experiences have been eye-openers and have led to several major initiatives, like this incident that she recounts, 'In one of those initial years of SEWA's financial lending services, twenty women defaulted on repayment of the loans. On realising this, we conducted a survey to ascertain the cause. Much to our dismay, we found that seventeen of them had died due to childbirth or accidents.' A woman of great sensibility and sensitivity, Elaben constituted a trust, introducing a maternity scheme for SEWA members. She contributed the full amount that she received as prize money of the Ramon Magsaysay Award in 1977, to this trust. Taking a cue from their leader, members of SEWA contributed anywhere between ₹7 to ₹35—an amount that equalled one day's wage, to this fund. This was followed by a scheme for social security of widows. Elaben's journey only became more and more rigorous as time elapsed. Her fight for a social security scheme saw fruition seven years ago, when Unorganised Workers' Social Security Act was passed at the ILO convention in 2008.

SEWA is not the only feather in her cap, she has sparked several other institutions like Sa-Dhan (All India Association of Microfinance Institutions), Indian School of Microfinance for Women, Women's World Banking, HomeNet (International Alliance of Home Based Workers) and Women in Informal Employment: Globalizing and Organizing (WIEGO). As a member of The Elders, she has worked alongside Nelson Mandela and continues to work with Kofi Annan, Martti Ahtisaari and Desmond Tutu and other global leaders for peace and human rights across the world. Both awards and smiles are plentiful when Elaben is around. She has received Global Fairness Initiative Award, Ramon Magsaysay Award, Padma Bhushan, Right Livelihood Award, George Meany-Lane Kirkland Human Rights Award, Légion d'honneur and a million smiles.

Elaben's '100 Mile' principle is an innovation that has aroused great intrigue and scholarly discussions the world over. 'The 100 Mile Principle urges us to meet life's basic needs with goods and services that are produced no more than 100 miles from where we live. This includes food, shelter, clothing, primary education, primary health care and primary banking. It also focuses on the ideas of community and citizenship.' When quizzed on why she chose 100 miles as the optimal distance, she says, 'One simple reason is that you can travel 100 miles and return home by dinner time. But 100 miles does not need to be taken literally—it represents the distance that can provide essential goods and services for a district or state. It could be 200 miles in a desert or hilly region, fifty miles in a dense, produce-rich location, or ten miles near a town. The distance of 100 miles is a starting point for thinking in local terms. The 100 Mile Principle ties decentralisation, locality, size and scale to livelihood, suggesting that the materials, energy, and knowledge that one needs to live should come from areas around us,' she explains.

Citing findings from Shakti Report, which she prepared after closely interacting with women in the unorganised labour force across eighteen states in India, she says, 'We found that women are actually more futuristic. They face the wrath of the world and the fury of nature better than men do. They are so very resourceful. A mother finds ways to feed her children, even in the worst famine or crisis. She is a worker, and a preserver. She builds the bond of relationships. She wants stability and strong roots for her children to grow from. These processes are slow, hence women may take time in proving it to the world. If you let them grow at their pace and add to their productivity, they are fearless. Their entrepreneurial spirit is high.'

—Priyanka Jain

left
The dexterity of fingers imparts finesse to the art of embroidery. There are diverse patterns and styles of sewing and embroidery in India, specific to each region. Besides providing employment opportunities to numerous women, it also contributes significantly to India's exports.

Peace in Paradise

Susheela Bhan, social activist and researcher

'If you ask me what I consider my greatest achievement in life, I would say I am proud of my work among school students in Kashmir. It opens up their minds and gives them a glimpse of new horizons. It is this, rather than the reams of research I have done, that makes me feel good about myself when I look back on my life,' says Susheela Bhan, director of the Institute of Peace Research and Action (IPRA), the first of its kind in the strife-stricken state of Kashmir. The 'Cultural Renewal of Kashmiri Youth' programme conducted by dedicated teams from IPRA, in the government schools of Kashmir, guides students and teachers in the rebuilding of a society with four core values: democracy, secularism, social justice and human rights.

Why is influencing young minds positively so important in Kashmir? Why is redirecting the energy of its youth crucial for a socio-cultural and economic turnaround of this land? Since the 1990s, it is Kashmir's school children who have been accessed as easy recruits for disparate militant groups. Consequently, school children are also the first victims of all armed groups in the Valley. 'The devastation around was incredible. I talked to people and they narrated the vivid details of the hell they had gone through. I returned to Delhi with a numbness and hopelessness I had never experienced before. But then, I knew I had to do something. I owed it to my people. The IPRA culture club project emerged as the only response I was capable of,' Susheela shares.

And she has been working tirelessly towards engaging the youth. Armed with the weapons of Kashmiriyat—the Kashmiri Sufi-based heritage that extols universal humanity and abhors intolerance and exploitation, and projects to induce a sense of achievement and skill development, she serves the youth of her home state with all compassion. Her programme has been taken up in more than 200 schools across half a dozen districts of Kashmir and encourages almost 300 different kinds of activities. It may have significantly contributed towards the fact that not a single student from any of these schools has been recruited by militants in recent years. She aims to involve around 200,000 students and their teachers, these people are in turn responsible for influencing everyone else in their state. Thus, it not only serves to empower the youth to make their own choices, but also enables them to make a difference in the lives of others in their state.

To unravel the sentiments that lie beneath Susheela Bhan's work, one has to understand where she comes from. She was born in Srinagar in Kashmir, where she spent the first two decades of her life. People who know how much she loves academic research will be surprised to learn that she never had a formal schooling, despite belonging to a Brahmin family with a tradition of learning. Instead, she was home schooled as per the instructions of her grandfather who aimed at making her a matriculate so that she could read and write. She then completed her graduation from a private college and embarked on her career as a lecturer in Political Science, in 1954 at the Government Degree College for Women. Her mother instilled in her the confidence that she had the potential to achieve whatever she desired. She and her sister were encouraged to question, argue and debate upon various issues of concern. 'I believe that education is not just about passing exams, it should bring about development of personality through exposure to society. This is what the culture clubs in the Valley aim to achieve,' Susheela Bhan says, reflecting upon her own experiences as a student in Kashmir.

Later on, with the timely intervention of her uncle, she was sent to the University of London for higher studies, where she studied for four years and registered to do two courses simultaneously at the Institute of Education and the School of Oriental and African Studies. Life and exposure to a new culture, a new society was unnerving for the naive girl she was, then. 'Steeped in conservative values, I remember the culture shock I experienced when I saw my professor dancing with the cleaning lady at a Christmas party in London. I also learnt as to what it meant to be an independent woman, especially when I moved out of the hostel into a shared flat

Kashmiri school girls playing rugby at Gulmarg, near Srinagar. Jammu and Kashmir tourism department has taken several measures to attract tourists, and this event held on the New Year's Eve is one of them. Steps have also been taken to ensure the safety and security of tourists, especially women.

in Chelsea.' On her return to India in 1970, she worked as professor of education at the College of Education, University of Srinagar. She joined the Indian Council of Social Science Research, an autonomous institution under the Ministry of Human Resource Development, in 1976 where she worked for eighteen years. She was awarded the prestigious Ashoka Fellowship by the Washington-based foundation in 2003. 'This gave me a chance to put what I knew about Kashmiri culture into action, which was quite an eye-opening experience,' she recalls. 'Now I am doing a sociological study of Kashmiri society, putting the sum of my experiences and observations in a book.' And that would be Susheela Bhan's sixth book, not to forget the fifty papers published in national and international journals. She has deftly dealt with a variety of issues including child abuse, criminalisation of politics and the scourge of terrorism.

'Kashmir will always be my home and the closest to my heart,' Susheela says, although her father sold his house in Srinagar and moved to Delhi. 'We left some of our belongings at my sister's house in Batamalloo, which was burnt down completely in 1993. That is how I lost all photographs of my childhood and early adult years. But I will never lose my value systems or belief in syncretic culture, because it is deeply embedded in us, in fact it is part of the pure air we breathe in the Himalayas and the society in which we spent the most impressionable years of our lives. When I visit my homeland for my work, and often visit my brother, it's as if I never went away from there,' she reminisces.

She admits there is a deeper satisfaction in going back to her roots, in using her knowledge of Kashmiri culture and identity to help youngsters free themselves from the anxiety about their future. The last half-a-decade has been a critical phase in the history of Kashmiris that led to the need for a serious attention towards stabilizing social, cultural and economic institutions of the Valley. The IPRA project, through programmes like debates, seminars, symposia etc. in schools provides opportunity to discover and rediscover structures of consciousness and a vision for Kashmir in the new millennium.

'Our cultural clubs in schools help teenagers optimise their talent and give them a chance to crystallise their worldview. My approach is to expose students to architectural sites, poets and Sufi saints. We teach them about Lalleshwari, a 14th century rebel against the repressive social order of her day, who rejected caste, ritual and religious discrimination. Telling them about inspirational figures from their own land gives them role models who are not remote or too exotic to emulate. My objective is...starting with the students and teachers, to transform the society into something dynamic, secular and plural, so that people will never be exploited again, so that they will fight for their rights,' Susheela says. Equipped with new attitudes, knowledge, and skills, students and teachers become a force for positive change, she explains.

She also focusses on advocacy and women's issues. A picture of poise and grace, seventy-year-old Susheela shares a good rapport with children in the Valley, and this gets IPRA easy access to their families. 'Girls are our most vulnerable citizens,

right
A young Kashmiri woman at the shrine of Shah-e-Hamdan, one of the oldest Muslim shrines in Jammu & Kashmir. Lalleshwari or Lal Ded, a mystic of the Kashmiri Shaivite sect, inspired some of the later Sufis of Kashmir. Her verses are the earliest compositions in the Kashmiri language and form an important part in the history of Kashmiri literature.

they need to be handled with sensitivity,' she avers. She fondly recalls a girl at one school who would wear a burkha throughout the whole day, refusing to take it off in class. A few months after Susheela encountered this student, a militant group threatened girls who failed to wear the burkha with death. The next time Susheela went to the school, she saw the same student without her burkha. When asked why she did not wear the burkha any more, Susheela was told, the local cultural club coordinator had explained how dress should be a matter of choice, not obligation. The student had discussed the matter with her father, who had agreed and advised her that morality is a reflection of a person's character, not clothes. Hence, she had chosen not to wear the burkha, concluding, 'I refuse to be pushed around by them. They don't know more about Islam than we do.'

'India is always lauded as a tolerant society. That is because we all live together despite all the cultural, religious and linguistic differences. I hope, in my own way, I am contributing to keeping the legacy alive,' Susheela Bhan says with all the wisdom of her years. Adding, 'I believe that building a tolerant and pluralistic society is not the task of the government alone—we citizens must seize the initiative if we are uniquely placed to do so.'

—Manjula Lal

right (top)
A Kashmiri school girl participates in the celebration of India's Independence Day at Bakshi Stadium in Srinagar.

right (bottom)
A mother and daughter delighting in festivities in Ladakh, one of the most thinly populated regions of Jammu and Kashmir. Ladakh is the highest plateau of Kashmir and attracts tourists from all over the world, owing to its culture and scenic beauty. The magnificent monasteries in Leh and Ladakh also play a major role in making it a tourist hotspot.

Driving Courage

Surekha Yadav, Asia's first motor woman

I f you thought a girl driving a Harley Davidson was cool, wait till you meet Surekha Yadav, Asia's first motor woman, who has driven every kind of train—from suburban local trains to goods trains, from long distance express trains to the twin engine 'ghat-loco' trains that ply through the Western Ghats. Her refreshing candour, modest civility and her presence itself redefines cool. 'I am a simple woman. It is not that things are any different just because I am a woman,' says Surekha. There is no outward machismo in her dressing—no pants, caps or expensive shoes that she adorns. It is easy for this petite forty-eight-year-old to merge into the hordes of women commuters on Indian Rail in her everyday salwar kurta, mangalsutra and neatly plaited shoulder length hair. But if you looked closely, you would notice the precision and the speed of her long strides with which she crosses twelve coaches on a crowded local railway platform in three minutes flat. 'Being quick is part of the training we receive when working towards becoming train drivers,' she says.

Even before you curiously inquire about the motivation behind her being in a male dominated profession, she cuts in, 'It is all about perception. It is our not wanting to try our hands at something that makes us eventually call any profession male-dominated. No one has stopped a woman from becoming a train driver or anything else that she wishes to be. If only a few women have the resolve to accomplish something challenging, and even fewer actually end up doing that; the perception of gender domination in such professions will never change. The onus is on the women to break the shell and come out in flying colours.'

These bold words don't stem out of the fact that she is now Asia's first motor woman, but out of the conviction that she nurtured much earlier in life. In fact, it was this that led her to take the wheels of the train! While enrolling into college for higher education, she desired to pursue a technical vocational elective, which required her to attend a boys' college for two days a week during the period of her course. 'When I told my principal, he said that no girl had done so till then, and he was not sure if the technical college would accept me attending their course. He asked me to go and talk to them.' Anxious, yet full of energy and confidence, she approached the principal of the technical college, who was bowled over by her enthusiasm and accepted her without picking a bone over her being the only girl in a batch of sixty-five boys. Despite the gender factor, she never felt out of place, and she says, 'Even as a child, I was never treated differently by my parents. They made sure that their three daughters and two sons were brought up in similar manner. They encouraged all of us to acquire a good education and never questioned our ambitions.'

Surekha says she never misused the freedom and trust her parents reposed in her. 'I was determined to reach the top in my field. With that goal in mind, I just kept working towards it every day.' She knew the qualifying examination to drive trains was a tough one and was happy when she cleared it, along with twenty-five others. 'When I cleared all three exams and got an appointment letter, I figured in the eligibility list of those selected to drive trains. I still had many around me trying to dissuade me from the rather unusual profession. But it would have been stupid of me to have come all this way and not taken up the challenge to drive the trains, so I jumped in.'

Her dedication and determination also saw her gaining support from her colleagues and seniors at work, all of whom were men. But she does miss having women companions at work and in her social life, and says, 'I miss the friendship of women. I almost feel shy talking with girls now.' Surekha says that women have much more capacity, tolerance and perseverance than men. Pointing to Rani Lakshmi Bai of Jhansi and Indira Gandhi as the greatest influences in her life, she adds, 'Women can multitask; we work outside and at home with equal success, but we underestimate ourselves. If we put our minds to it, we can do anything.' However, she does admit that she has to be on the toes at her job, which keeps her glued to work even during odd hours. She, therefore, gets to spend lesser time than she would have liked to, with her two teenaged sons and her police-officer husband. Yet, Surekha takes pride in the fact that she never allowed her career choices let her family life suffer. She says, 'I have done only two things in life—I have done my job and taken care of my home. I don't know anything else about the world outside. I sometimes miss having a girl child.'

Surekha says that her job requires a keen sense of observation, patience, concentration, quick decision-making, alertness, discipline and resilience in

left
Surekha Yadav at Chhatrapati Shivaji Terminus in Mumbai. She believes that handling the great responsibility of driving a train full of people safely to their destinations has nothing to do with gender. It is about patience, concentration, quick decision-making, alertness, discipline and resilience.

abundance, regardless of gender. How to inculcate all this, and tackle emotional stress while faced with trying situations at work, is what she teaches her students at the Railways Motorman Training School, where she is currently posted. She also notes that women in general tend to become careless about their own selves and rarely attend to their health needs. 'There are two things I tell my students to sort out, as soon as they feel unwell. One is, when you feel tired or sick, see a doctor immediately and get it fixed. Rest enough and take on only as much work as you can do. And the other thing is, to not worry about issues that are of no concern to you. When you devote your energies worrying about stray issues, the important issues take a back seat and you are left empty handed.' Surekha feels that teaching future train drivers has made her stay up to date and brush up on the finest nuances and technicalities of her profession.

Though she finds her current assignment of being a mentor 'fascinating', having worked in the field for twenty-two years, her heart lies in being in the driver's seat. Surekha worked as an assistant driver from 1989 to 1994 on trains to Kalyan and Lonavala, before she got promoted as a goods driver assistant in 1996. In 1999, she was an independent driver on a goods train and had assistants under her. On 14 April 2000, after completing her motorman training for local trains, she drove her first passenger local from CST to Dombivali. Then in 2011, she got her first long distance train—the Deccan Queen. 'I have been receiving appreciation since the day I got into this job, but I still feel overwhelmed when so much love, smiles and bouquets come my way.' It has been twenty-five years since Surekha embarked on this steaming journey, and today, Indian Railways has eleven women drivers in its fold.

Surekha confides that on her first brush with the engine, she experienced a mix of fear and excitement, like any other driver. 'I just wanted the train and passengers to reach safely and on time.' She says being the first motor woman in Asia came with a bag of responsibilities. 'To drive a crowded train safely and on time is a huge responsibility. If a driver does the job vigilantly, follows the signals correctly, and keeps her head cool while troubleshooting in case of any complication—the job is well done. Sometimes, if the train is late, people hurl abuses, but you learn to take that in your stride.' When asked about how passengers respond on seeing a woman behind the wheels, she says, 'Sometimes, during emergencies, people discover that there is a woman driver. I don't lose my cool, whatever be their response. And if the mob is angry, it generally calms down a bit when people spot a woman driver at the controls.'

She says, 'While it can be frustrating to struggle with a defective motor and repair it in a matter of minutes to ensure the timely arrival of the train, the mental blow that an accident can strike can't be expressed in words.' These eventualities, she says, are a part of her job. 'I have to pull up my socks, keep my calm and be normal within minutes because despite the occurrence, I can't afford to take a break in the journey. I have to complete the run of the train's course,' she adds.

right
A train halted at Barog station, at the narrow gauge railway line between Kalka and Shimla. UNESCO recognises Shimla-Kalka Mountain Railway as a 'World Heritage Site' which has also been described as one of the most 'authentic mountain railways in the world'.

Her fitness philosophy also makes one smile. Since she worked odd hours, it was difficult to find a domestic help to pitch in during the time she would spent at home, thus, she would end up doing all the household chores on her own. 'The movements and physical activities involved in cooking, cleaning the house, utensils and washing clothes double up as the requisite exercise to ensure my physical fitness,' she says.

—Priyanka Jain

Power-packed Performer

Teejan Bai, folk-artiste

The song ends, applause rings loudly around the room, her fans clamour around her. But what is it that makes Teejan Bai such a hit amongst her audience? Is it her deep-throated drawl, her colourful bangles, vermillion and *bindi* on her forehead, or is it the magic of the music she creates?

'When I enact the *cheer-haran* of Draupadi, I become the strong Bhim and the fierce Dushasan. Once in a while, I break into a dance move while singing the epic.' Teejan Bai needs no introduction for those familiar with folk culture of India. For the uninitiated, she is an iconic exponent of Pandavani, a folk dance and music form, which has its roots in the Indian heartland state of Chhattisgarh. Looking back at her career that spans over more than four decades, the sixty-three-year-old woman still sings with élan and mesmerises audiences cutting across languages. She personifies the coming of age of the Pandavani art form and is a quintessential bridge between the ancient folk music and modernity. Pandavani is a spectacular and theatrical narration of the *Mahabharata* by the tribal folk of Chhattisgarh. While narrating the epic, the narrator becomes the protagonist. Roughly ten times the length of the *Iliad* and the *Odyssey* combined, with a narrative of 1.8 million words, the *Mahabharata* is the longest epic poem in the world and many a times described as the 'longest poem ever written'.

Teejan Bai created history when she was just thirteen years old, as a Pandavani singer under the guidance of her maternal grandfather, Brijlal Pardhi. She is not just the first woman to take this up, but also the one who reached zenith in her craft.

'The male-dominated style of Pandavani, known as the Kapalik, always interested me and inspired me to take it up as a career. The Vedamati style, usually performed by women, is a less lively form,' says Teejan Bai. She sings with an unmistakable masculine verve, challenging the hitherto male bastion. 'I was ostracised—thrown out of my house at thirteen for singing the Pandavani. My prospective in-laws told my father that they needed a daughter-in-law who could cook, not one who sang. I left home and went to the nearby village where my other band members had gone for a performance. I joined them and started earning my bread and butter. The key is to never give up,' she says.

Soon, people started recognising Teejan Bai for her work. Neighbouring villages started inviting her for performances. Once her parents went to a nearby village to catch a glimpse of her performance and were left spell bound on seeing her enact the Pandavani characters. 'After the show ended, I met my parents and they decided to take me back home.' Pandavani became her life and career right after her first performance.

Soon she met Unmed Singh Deshmukh, a Pandavani artiste, and began taking formal training from him. She learnt the entire epic by heart and a chain of performances followed one after the other. Her powerful rendition of the epic, her rustic charm and simplicity made her immensely popular not only in Chhattisgarh, but everywhere in India and abroad. From Kashmir to Kanyakumari and Gujarat to Bengal, she has managed to captivate the people of India by her performance. She has also enchanted large crowds in almost all parts of the world by her performances in places like France, Switzerland, Germany, Italy, Britain, England, Turkey, Tunisia, Malta, Cyprus, Romania, Yemen, Bangladesh and Mauritius.

Talking about the traditional instrument that she carries in one hand, Teejan Bai says 'One thing that has stood by me in thick and thin is the tamboora. When nobody was by my side, in poverty and in wealth, the tamboora has always been my partner. While the strings are the throne of Goddess Saraswati, if you add peacock feathers to it, it represents Lord Krishna, and it even assumes the role of Lord Hanuman.'

No matter how ill she is, she never postpones her performances. She feels, singing the Pandavani gives her strength and keeps her healthy. 'I remember an instance where I had fractured my leg. I spoke to the organisers, but they said it was difficult for them to cancel or postpone the show. I was helped by my team members, stood at the centre of the stage and got down only after the performance came to an end. There are times, when I have high fever, I take medicines and get on the stage.

left
Teejan Bai sharing her experience of keeping the Pandavani art form alive, at Sphoorthi Theatre in Hyderabad.

This has been my attitude towards Pandavani and I do not think it is going to change anytime soon.'

'I've never wanted to do anything else. I am living with this art form and will die with it,' says this iron-willed icon of modern India, who is also an officer at the Bhilai Steel Plant, and strongly believes in hard work and determination.

Born to Chunuk Lal Pardhi and Sukhwati, in a small village of Ganiyari in 1956, Teejan is a woman full of strength, courage, confidence and dedication today, able to charge huge audiences with a single gesture or the raising of an eyebrow.

'In spite of facing rejection a few times in my life, I am now a proud homemaker, wife, mother, grandmother and a professional artiste,' Teejan Bai says that the one thing she still regrets is not being able to go to school. She firmly believes that if she could reach such heights of skill and success being uneducated, she could have reached an unimaginable level, had she been educated. Her Padma Shri came in the year 1988 and Padma Bhushan in the year 2003. She received the Sangeet Natak Akademi Award in 1995 and Alva's Vishwa Virasat Award in 2013. Teejan Bai also has four doctorates. 'Being academically challenged, I always thought a doctor is only someone who prescribes medicines. The fact that a person can be honoured with a doctorate without medical knowledge took me time to understand. And today, I have reached a stage where I will be honoured with a doctorate for the fourth time, in January 2014,' she confides, adding that education is a must for the girl child.

'I have had some 150-200 students so far. Every year, when I am on a visit to other states of India or other countries, I conduct workshops and teach them. This has become a part of my life now. This is my small effort towards keeping this dance and music form alive in the hearts of Indians. My students will help preserve this tradition,' adds Teejan Bai.

Beneath the layers of make-up, she is just a simple woman, who adores and cares about her husband, children and grandchildren. She goes out of her way to help the people living in her neighbourhood financially. 'My childhood was replete with dramatic turns. I was made to give up my passion, so many times. But that helped me mature into an artiste,' she says.

'Pandavani has given me a career, an identity, and love and respect of thousands of followers. It has also given me a positive outlook towards life and the strength of character. The least I owe Pandavani is to remain surrendered to this wonderful art form and to pray to the gods that I am able to keep performing till the last breath of my life.'

—Pooja Mehta

bottom
Pandavani artists don traditional clothes and elaborate jewellery which add to the impact of their performance.

right
Teejan Bai performing at an event, her tamboora (the one-string instrument) raised high above her head. She believes that only four instruments are necessary to promote Pandavani—tabla, harmonium, tamboora and damru. Several times, as the performance progresses, the tamboora becomes her only prop, which she then uses to personify the characters she portrays.

The Winning Edge

Saina Nehwal, badminton player

'One thought—to win!' she declares. 'That is the only thought in my head and heart when I step into the badminton court. The shuttlecock is my target, the racket is my tool, and winning is my only goal.' That is Saina Nehwal for you—India's youngest sportswoman who has carved an enviable niche for herself in the world of badminton, carrying the pride of the nation on her shoulders. 'Intelligence and grit is what is required on the ground. Hard work and God's grace alone can take you through it. There is no substitute for hard work,' she says, when asked about her secret to success.

Saina Nehwal, the twenty-three-year-old champ, winner of India's first ever Olympic Medal in badminton, first Indian to win the World Junior Badminton Championship and the Super Series Tournament…and the list goes on, when one gets to array her achievements till date. And one can be doubly sure that the list will get populated at a brisk rate, in the years to come. 'I was just an ordinary child, he made me the badminton player I am today,' she says of her mentor and renowned badminton player Pullella Gopichand, her unassuming smile overshadowed by the glow of reverence in her eyes for her coach. In 1999, while in Hyderabad, young Saina was spotted by SM Arif, the Dronacharya award winning badminton coach, and he unearthed the hidden talent in her. Since then, that has been her only focus; the whole and soul of Saina Nehwal.

Saina was born in Hisar district of Haryana, where she spent most of her childhood. Soon, the family shifted to Hyderabad, where she spent her teenage years. She attributes her inability to make strong bonds of friendships at that age to this relocation of her family. And before she even realised it, she had already fallen in love—with badminton! In 2006, the sixteen-year-old Saina burst on to the national stage by bagging the under-nineteen national championship and went on to bring home the prestigious Asian Satellite Badminton medal consecutively for the second year. She also created history by becoming the first Indian woman to win a super-series tournament, the Philippines Open, and won the bronze medal at the Commonwealth Games. Over the years, there has hardly been any tournament the world over that has not been bagged by this golden girl of badminton from India. It is awe-inspiring to see the young starlet pile up awards in the merit of the Padma Shri, the Rajiv Gandhi Khel Ratna Award, and secure a place in the Forbes 100 Most Influential Indians List and a Rank 2 in the World Badminton Federation list of players in 2010, and yet remain rooted and unfazed by all the limelight that comes her way.

Having won the Bronze medal at London Olympics 2012, her eyes are now set on winning the Olympic Gold next, her focus fixed, and the intensity of training furious, 'I am very disciplined at the training sessions. I always reach fifteen minutes before the starting time. I cannot stay away from the badminton court for even a day. My parents were good players too. It's probably there in my genes…' she chuckles, referring to her parents Harvir Singh and Usha Nehwal, both former badminton champions for the state of Haryana. Having seen several highs and lows in her career, she realises that the power to climb to the top and stay there is no child's play. She says, 'My mother motivated me to push my limits in the game. My coaches helped me excel and my parents gave me the much-needed support and encouragement to opt for badminton as my career. When hurdles popped up in my way, my parents took care of them and ensured that my days were hassle-free. If all parents were to protect and look after the innate needs of their children just like my parents did, excellent results are bound to follow.' Her rigorous badminton training schedules of two sessions per day, apart from physical fitness regimes hardly leaves any space or time for her to engage herself with the world outside the game. However, she does make time for a spicy bite of aloo paratha, her hot favourite from her mother's kitchen, while feasting her eyes on her next favourite—a Shahrukh Khan starrer Hindi movie.

As a young woman achiever that the nation looks up to, Saina presents a very positive picture about her life, as she says, 'As a woman, I did not face any specific challenges, nor did I ever have to prove myself extra hard. By God's grace, I think that being in the right place at the right time also worked in my favour.' She would love to be of help to younger sportswomen in India, who she thinks have tremendous

left
Saina Nehwal during the award ceremony of women's singles final against Wang Shixian of China at the Hong Kong Open Super Series 2010. She won 2-1 to claim the championship.

page 75
Saina competes against Wang Xin of China during the quarter-final in the 2011 Sudirman Cup in Qingdao. She won 2-0. Like Saina carried forward the legacy of her mentor, P Gopichand, winner of All England Open Badminton Championships in 2001, PV Sindhu, a rising star, is carrying the baton forward.

page 76
Saina Nehwal looks up after winning against China's Wang Shixian during the All England Open Badminton Championship women's singles quarter-final match in Birmingham, England, in 2013.

potential to scale great heights. 'I am very lucky and happy to be a woman, a sportsperson, and an Indian. I believe in the bright future of the nation and consider today's children to be invaluable assets for nation building. The girl child is more special, and needs to be nurtured and cared for,' she asserts.

Saina does think that sports other than cricket are not being given their rightful place in India. But that is not to say that she doesn't love cricket, or any other sport, for that matter. When asked who inspires her the most, she utters three names: 'In tennis, Roger Federer is my favourite. I respect him a lot and love watching him play. Sachin Tendulkar in cricket and Taufik Hidayat in badminton are my favourites. I respect all these players. They have changed my life and I take a lot of inspiration from them.' She knows that there are many young girls and boys who look up to her, just the way she admires these stars and confesses, 'I sometimes feel like a film star now.' And her advice to the aspiring players amongst them is, 'Work hard and be prepared for tough training. It's not easy. It is a difficult game. If you really believe in yourself, you can do it. If I can do it, you can do it too. Work hard and keep going.'

—Radhika Rajamani

Agniputri: Born of Fire

Tessy Thomas, missile scientist

The quintessential symbol of feminine strength as represented in the Indian epics, Draupadi is said to have been born of fire; Agnijyotsna, as she is called in the *Mahabharata*. Her travails and triumphs continue to instil a fiery spirit in the daughters of India. The modern nation state has found its own Agniputri in the feisty scientist and missile developer, Tessy Thomas. 'Dr APJ Kalam is my guru in this field. He was my director at Defence Research and Development Organisation (DRDO) when I joined. I have been with the Agni programme since 1988...and have had the privilege to design the guidance programmes for all the Agni missiles,' she says. When asked how she feels about being called the Missile Woman of India, in professional comparison with her guide and former President of India, popularly known as the Missile Man of India, her modesty surpasses her ebullience, 'I feel happy and proud when people refer to me as the Agniputri or Missile Woman of India. But there is simply no comparison between me and him. He is a great personality, whereas I am only a beginner, even at this stage.'

This forty-nine-year-old scientist spearheaded India's most illustrious Intercontinental Ballistic Missile Programme—the Agni. After successfully test-firing the over-5000 km range Agni-V missile recently, Tessy has now set her eyes upon a canister-based launch for the missile, and to further develop the indigenous warhead Multiple Independently Targetable Re-entry Vehicle (MIRV). Having been acknowledged by the Prime Minister of India at the Indian Science Congress in January 2012, where he said, 'Dr Tessy is an example of a woman making her mark in a traditionally male bastion and decisively breaking the glass ceiling', she attributes her success in the field to the non-discriminatory nature of science as a discipline, 'I see no gender discrimination in science, as science doesn't know who is working for it. When I reach the office, I am no more in the role of a woman. I am a scientist. No matter what your gender, race, caste or any other barrier that is a social construct, science is beyond all those.'

However, she does admit that it was a rather unusual choice to be made in those days, to enter the male dominated sphere of defence research. And she is more than glad to see that her steps in the right direction have significantly contributed to balancing out the gender bias at DRDO, where, over the course of a quarter century that she has been associated with the organisation, the percentage of women scientists have quadrupled from 2-3 per cent to 12-15 per cent. She also strongly believes that sincerity and dedication towards your work irons out all differences. 'When you are not in a majority, you are bound to face a lot of hurdles. You do your work sincerely and you will get good results, along with wider acceptance,' says Tessy.

Her work and journey has borne testimony to the poised and down-to-earth achiever in her. It all started in 1985, when Tessy was selected as one amongst the ten meritorious youngsters from across the country, for a DRDO programme. It was then that she met Dr Kalam, who took notice of her project on 'gyro-less inertial navigation' that she had worked on during her post-graduate studies, and deputed her to work on the Agni series of missiles, for which she eventually designed the guidance scheme. 'He created a great forum for exchange of ideas and all of us have benefitted from that,' she fondly recollects.

By then, she already knew that she had chosen a great field of work, and that she had the right aptitude for it. Tessy had completed her Bachelors in Engineering from the Trichur Engineering College in Kerala, and went on to do her Masters in Guided Missile Technology at the Institute of Armament Technology in Pune, which has since become the Defence Institute of Advanced Technology (DIAT), a decision that took her career and life to the next level. The DIAT stint did not just present her with the glorious professional life that followed, but also a cherished family life that she is extremely grateful for.

She met her husband Saroj Patel, who belonged to a different religion and region, during her days at the institute. On how exciting were those moments of exchange of warmth, she gushes, 'During our studies, we were not even aware of the fact that we had actually fallen in love. It was only after both of us had completed the course, that he proposed to me. Though my parents are dedicated Syrian Christians, they created no fuss and said I could marry him as long as his parents didn't have any

objections either.' Tessy finds her most ardent supporter in her husband, who is now a Commodore in the Indian Navy. They have a son, who has curiously been named Tejas. Though people often deem the name to be a choice made after Tejas—India's light combat aircraft by the over-enthusiastic scientist in her, she chuckles away as she confesses that his name was derived from an anagram of the names of her husband and herself.

She delights in her duties as a wife and mother, despite her nerve-wracking sixteen-hour work schedules, day after day. 'I enjoy cooking a lot. I used to wake up early in the morning, cook for the entire family and, come back late evening and serve dinner. Now my husband is in Mumbai and my son in Tamil Nadu, so I just cook for myself and carry my lunch along to work,' she says in a way only a mother could. Tessy indulges in a game of badminton or an hour before the television watching soap operas, when she feels the need to take a break and unwind. There have been instances when she has felt the crunch, juggling with the demands of her profession and needs of her family. 'Indian culture asks of a woman to devote much time and space of her life to her family. It was particularly difficult when my son was younger and in school.' It has all been worth it though, she feels, as she now sees a son who understands her predicaments, is extremely proud of his mother's achievements and aspires to be like her someday.

She learnt the art of dealing with challenges and obstacles in life from her own mother, Kunjamma Thomas. Tessy was born in the picturesque town of Alappuzha, which carries the epithet of Venice of the East, as one of five sisters and a brother. She was named Tessy after Mother Teresa. She doesn't find any contradiction in the mission that her parents thought she would emulate and the mission of defence projects that life has set out for her. 'The missiles we develop are weapons of peace. A country needs to be strong enough to deter malevolent forces from attacking it. If we are prepared for war, peace ensues,' Tessy asserts. With a glint in her eyes, she remembers her rather unexceptional childhood. 'I was like any other village child who went to school, enjoyed life, came back and played. And I used to love science and maths as a student.'

Misfortune struck them when she was in Class VIII, when her father TJ Thomas had a paralytic attack. Since then, he was confined to a bed until he passed away in 1991. She recalls how as children, they were inspired by their mother, who raised them single-handedly, even as she took care of their father. 'My mother was a qualified teacher, but chose to not take it up as a profession. She spent all her time teaching the six of us. She had the will power to look after my ailing father as well as all of us. Today, she is seventy-five and as a mother, she continues to inspire all of us.' She does miss her father. In remembrance, she says, 'My father was very good at mathematics and a very knowledgeable person. He was the one who encouraged me to take up engineering. All my crucial choices in life have seen his unfailing support. I really miss him.'

'He would have been the happiest person to see the laurels that I receive today,' signs off the faithful daughter whose achievements are aplenty, including the DRDO Award for Path Breaking Research/Outstanding Technology Development and the Lal Bahadur Shastri National Award.

—Divya S Iyer, Cynthia Chandran

right (top)
A young scientist at work inside India's missile lab in Hyderabad. India became the sixth nation to have the inter-continental ballistic missile technology.

right (bottom)
Women scientists from the Indian Space Research Organisation (ISRO) work in the Indian Regional Navigational Satellite System (IRNSS) control room at the Indian Deep Space Network (IDSN), a network of large antennas and communication facilities that supports India's interplanetary spacecraft missions, located at Byalalu village about 50 kms from Bengaluru.

page 81-82
India's Mars bound rocket and satellite blasted off in November 2013 from Sriharikota in Andhra Pradesh. India's rendezvous with the red planet Mars has begun with its $100 million mission—Mangalyaan. The women at ISRO, almost 2500 of them, are contributing significantly to the success of its various missions in fulfilling the national needs.

Guns, Granny & Glory

Chandro Tomar, the oldest professional woman shooter

The fog sits thick over the landscape, a warm blanket, even as Dadi Chandro steps out of the darkness and ushers me in, to her CFL-lit room. I am in a twilight world, having just come from a 150-year-old *haveli* running wild and donated by the village overlord where the sports authorities in India have set up a shooting range at a cost of ₹2.5 million. A place which has given the country some of its best shots, many young women among them. Their inspiration, Chandro Tomar, the village grandmother who is believed to be the oldest professional woman sharpshooter!

The eighty-year-old woman in a blue *ghagri* lives in Jauri village on the road to Meerut, going into the heart of western Uttar Pradesh. Here, urbanisation is swiftly making inroad into a predominantly sugarcane-growing rural economy; tractors move alongside camels, mud tracks are being macadamised, 600-people villages turning into 6,000-people small towns that dot the district.

An outrider on a motorbike had led me into the village and through a narrow paved alleyway lined by exposed brick houses, to a blue painted door, as dusk descended. Inside, as I cross a cobbled courtyard, I can see large single rooms, with single bulbs, in the faint moonlight. The smell of cattle overwhelms me as the feisty old lady leads me to her den. Her room is large, faded photos lining the shelves cut in the walls and low sofas, with a glass-topped table, on which she spread out the newspaper clippings that carry her story. The story of how an unlettered elderly village woman with just household skills became a champion airgun and pistol shooter, brought fame to her nondescript village and in the process, transformed her village into one that provides a stream of young men and women who defend some of the crucial security services of the nation.

Picking up a framed photograph from the niche behind her, Chandro Tomar wipes it with her *dupatta* and laughs, 'He stopped me, but he never *actually* stopped me. Had he really stopped me, I would not have been the ace shooter that I am.' The 'he' Dadi Chandro is talking about was her farmer husband Bhanvar Singh. It was 1997 and Chandro was a sixty-five-year-old grandma and her husband was older. And he didn't 'really, really' stop her from shooting, a range sport that a local club and a village benefactor, Rajpal Singh, was trying to popularise at the time. Rajpal is a former international shooter.

'Rajpal wanted the children of this village to learn to shoot. This, he felt, would engage the young people and keep them focused on activities that would develop their skills, outside of school. He told my son, who was a village chief, to send his daughter to the club to learn. The child was nervous and I went with her. When it was her turn, she found it difficult to load the gun, so I did it for her. Soon, as the children learnt, I too did. And when they asked me to shoot, I did, and hit the bullseye at the very first try.'

Village mentor Rajpal Singh says he inherited the Indian Guru-Shishya philosophy. 'I studied in a gurukul, a traditional school, where teachers are the former students, handing over skills from one generation to the next. I am a shooting coach. I just got the village elders together and we decided to hand over this skill to the future generations. When we began teaching the village kids to shoot, I did not aim to create Arjunas. I wanted to create Ekalavyas—people who excel by drawing from their inner strength. Dadi Chandro is an example. Even today, and at her age, she travels to other places, from Tamil Nadu to Bihar, Chhattisgarh and Rajasthan, to train young people—her achievement, their biggest inspiration.'

There is pride in her voice as Dadi Chandro continues with her story in Khariboli, 'I practiced at the range and the children, the patrons and teachers at the club encouraged me. I told them I would practice with them, but they should not tell anyone at my home, or in the village.'

'I was very keen, so I began practising at home. My family had fifty members at the time. All of us lived under one roof. When everyone was asleep, I would fill a jug with water and hold it steady for hours at eye level. This steadied my hand, built the muscles in my arm.' Chandro Tomar brings out the big steel jug from a cupboard to show me. She also shows me all her weapons and her array of medals earned in the last fourteen years of her life. 'Once my pictures were in the local papers after

left
Chandro Tomar training at her village in Baghpat district in Uttar Pradesh. She has won over twenty-five national championships—a feat that becomes even more remarkable, considering the fact that she picked up a gun for the first time only about a decade ago.

I began to win contests, it was no longer a secret. People would say, "Oh! She is the lady from the village leader's house...or oh! She is our daughter-in-law's mother!" when they saw me in the papers.' Her first competition was the North Zone Air Pistol Championship in Chandigarh. Later, she went on to win the State National Championship medal; about twenty-five national-level medals decorate her much-worn shirt, her top honour a national Bronze.

Her son Vinod and daughter Savita, who are my hosts, add their voices to their champion mother's. 'If she goes to her village, Makhbulpur near Kandhla, people gather in hundreds to greet her. They say, this is the village where Chandro grew up.' Chandro says when she was young, her four brothers had guns, but she was scared to handle them then. 'I grew up with lots of love and affection. In those days, girls were married young; I was married at fifteen. Soon, my courtyard was filled with six young children. I had housework—milching cattle, weeding and sowing in the fields. My life was full, busy and content. Later, my sons too owned guns. I cleaned them, but never dreamt of firing one. Accompanying my granddaughters, I learnt to shoot. My sons supported me. They said, "Amma, don't shoot for winning competitions. Shoot for pleasure, because it satisfies you." My sons have been my pillars of support. I could, therefore, ignore all criticism and remain steady in my resolve and steadfast in my aim. *Muh mein Ram, haath mein kaam,* God's name on my lips and a gun in my hand,' Chandro adds.

'At one point of time, there were a dozen shooters in my family alone. The kids of this village, all who learnt to shoot, now have jobs with the army, the police, Border Security Force, Indian Airlines, security agencies and hotels. I ask the children to work hard—work in the fields, do housework, sweep, swab, hew, carry—so that they develop stamina. I feel proud when they do just that and win on the ranges.' Neetu, a grand niece, represented India in Hungary and Germany while twenty-seven other children from Jauri are international champions. From just farming, a different kind of prosperity has touched Dadi Chandro's village. Farming is the mainstay of this village, but its children dream of being on world stage, inspired by the village grandmother.

Tea break in the narrative means a steaming hot glass full of fresh sweetened milk. The washroom is sparkling clean, has modern facilities, electricity and running water. I realise the electrification and total sanitation campaign that India is advocating is very successful in this village. As I emerge, a calf under a spreading margossa sniffs at me while the smell of freshly baked chapattis wafts out of a tile-roofed kitchen. 'Education,' she says, 'is the biggest transforming force. It is education that has made all the difference in this village—awareness comes with education.' As I leave Dadi Chandro's bastion, the dense fog envelopes me, comforting me with the thought that from an indifferent past, Dadi Chandro's legacy is a bright future for not only the young in her village, but for the entire country.

—Papri Sri Raman

right
Indian Shooter Avneet Sidhu *(top)* and Tejaswini Sawant *(bottom)* at the Commonwealth Games in Melbourne in 2006, where they won a silver and gold (respectively) in Women's 10m Air Rifle Singles and a gold in Women's 10m Air Rifle Pairs, teamed together. Indian women shooters have performed consistently well in international championships.

Lap of Honour

Alisha Abdullah, India's fastest woman bike racer

She is said to have started enjoying the vroom of engines, the intoxicating smell of petrol and the exhilarating power of speed even before she was born. 'I would say my interest in racing started when I was in my mother's womb. My mother used to go and watch my father race when she was expecting me. When she was surrounded by the smell of petrol and the sound of racing engines, how could I not be interested in racing?' says Alisha Abdullah, India's fastest woman bike racer.

As a tiny tot, Alisha could often be found with her father at his races, even helping him dress for the races. 'I was like a tomboy on the track with him. But I never told him that some day, I too wanted to be a racer.' It is her father RA Abdullah, a famous bike racer and seven-time national champion, who Alisha considers her hero and role model.

She might have been crazy about cars and speed, but people looked at her as another little girl who loved dolls. 'I used to get Barbie dolls as gifts, but my interest was in buying these small cars which were called Hot Wheels then. I loved lining them up in a row and then racing them. It may sound weird, but racing cars gave me a high even then.' Today, twenty-four-year-old Alisha Abdullah is India's only woman super-bike racer, and the fastest woman car racer.

When a go-karting track was opened in Chennai, nine-year-old Alisha was there on the first day itself. 'I can never forget the day, not because I raced well, but because my hair got caught in the engine, as I had kept it open. My hair got pulled so hard that I ended up having a minute fracture. I started crying loudly, and my dad had to cut my hair to set me free. Then, he asked me to go back and race again. I cried and asked him, "What if something else happens?" He looked into my eyes and said, "Nothing will happen." I went back and drove faster and faster and faster. That incident taught me one thing—whatever happens, I should not give up. I should try till I succeed. I never felt scared on a racing track again.'

The go-karting track was her training ground and experimentation lab. 'I was the only girl, and I remember guys bullying me a lot. They used to gang up against me. They couldn't accept the fact that there was this girl trying to race with them. Fighting with the guys took a toll on me. After every race, I used to come home crying. It took me six to seven years to come out of the emotional drubbing they gave me every time I got on the track. I still remember the days when I first started racing on the 650cc super bikes. Initially, I used to really trail behind and finish last. One day, a guy chided me, "Are you not ashamed of performing like this? You are a shame on your father. You should get married and rear children. Bikes are not for you!"'

It hurt her so badly, that she locked herself up in her room and wept for hours. For the next weekend race, she practised very hard and stood third among twenty-five boys. 'This is for all the guys who put me down all the time. I thank each and every man who insulted me,' she proudly proclaimed on the podium. She believes that the tough get going and says, 'If I am a tough racer today, it is all because of those guys who bullied me mercilessly. My revenge is on the tracks.'

Life as a woman racer among macho men may not have been easy, but with experience, she has learned to tackle them with courage and speed. She gives credit to her father for being a pillar of support. 'Whenever I felt low, my father was the person who cheered me up. He was not just my father, but my coach and guide too,' says Alisha, getting ready to go international in April 2014 with the Asian Touring Cars series that takes place across several Asian countries, after making history in India.

It was not a natural transition for Alisha from bike racing to car racing. 'On a Valentine's day, I had a very bad fall from the bike, which left me unconscious for two hours. People thought that I was dead. For two years, I was in pain. After that, in 2010, I decided to move to car racing,' says the girl who chooses MotoGP over Formula 1, the Suzuka track in Japan for bikes and Silverstone in the UK for racing cars.

'Racing cars is very different. On the bikes, the gears are on your left foot and the brake on the right foot, but in cars, gears are in your hand. I had trained for years to race bikes and there is a lot of difference in the way you train for both. So, initially I used to come last in the races. But I soon became the first girl in the world to finish on the podium in Volkswagen,' she explains enthusiastically. The Volkswagen-J K Tyres Polo R Cup 2012 saw drama at the Kari Motor Speedway, Coimbatore when this

left
Alisha Abdullah, India's only woman super bike racer, is also the fastest Indian woman car racer. Apart from her father, Alisha draws inspiration from Mary Kom. She is a fan of Virat Kohli, the Indian cricketer, and admires his attitude and focus towards the game.

page 89
Alisha Abdullah has been called India's first female 'speed demon' at times. Although a cricket fan herself, she believes that other sports must be given equal importance. She expresses her happiness about boxing being noticed in the country, 'It's nice to see boxing come into the limelight, thanks to Mary Kom.'

page 90
In 2008, India became one of the seven countries to hold a license for a Formula One team. Force India is an Indian F1 team, one of the eleven F1 teams in the world. A woman of Indian origin, Monisha Kaltenborn, the principal of Sauber Formula One, is the first woman F1 team principal.

coveted championship witnessed the only female driver, Alisha Abdullah, leading the pack with 45 points.

She is still a lone woman racer at all the races, but she says, 'I don't feel out of place at all; it is the men who feel out of place. Whenever I overtake a guy, he feels insulted. I don't know why. I have heard them say, "Oh no, I have been overtaken by a girl!"'

The honour, though, is not easily earned. Most of Alisha's waking hours are spent in training. Does she miss going for movies, hanging out with friends and having a boyfriend? 'I also would like to have a life outside of racing, but I realised soon that this is the life I have chosen for myself. My boyfriend is my car. Racing is my love and my passion. I get tears in my eyes when I see a super car. I blush if I see a stylish racing car!'

Growing up as the only daughter of a Christian mother and a Muslim father was tough, she admits. 'It is very hard and complicated, though I get good clothes and good food for both Eid and Christmas! I used to go to the Church every Sunday and also prayed to Shirdi Sai Baba earlier. I have visited Shirdi too. But I found it very difficult to manage two religions, and my mother understood my confusion. So I decided to be a practising Muslim this Eid.'

Not to forget, speed, too, is like a religion for her. 'Speed, to me, is like a diamond that has to be used very carefully. I cannot afford to lose the diamond. If I misuse it a little, it will be gone forever. In fact, I want to spread the love and respect for speed. My dream is to open a racing training camp where I can train girls. After that, I want to have an all-girl racing team. Because there is no stopping a girl who knows where she is headed!'

—Shobha Warrier

On Top of the World

Bachendri Pal, first Indian woman on Mt Everest
Arunima Sinha, first woman amputee on Mt Everest

'Whatever experience I have gained, I want to share with the younger generation; for character building, to be courageous, independent, enterprising, and to believe in themselves so that they know their full potential. Most importantly, never to look for shortcuts and easy options,' such wisdom, which is bound to benefit enthusiastic learners, flows freely from the sixty-year-old mountaineer—Bachendri Pal, the first Indian woman to scale Mount Everest. She writes of her daring stretch of conquest in her memoir—*Everest: My Journey to the Top:* 'And at 1:07 pm on 23 May, 1984, I stood on top of Everest—becoming the first Indian woman to have done so. There was hardly enough place for two to stand side by side on top of the Everest cone. Thousands of metres of near vertical drop on all sides made safety our foremost consideration and we first anchored ourselves securely by digging our ice-axes into the snow. That done, I sank to my knees, and putting my forehead on the snow, kissed Sagarmatha's crown. Without getting up, I took out the image of Durga Maa and my Hanuman Chalisa from my rucksack. I wrapped these in a red cloth which I had brought and, after saying a short prayer, buried them in the snow. At this moment of joy, my thoughts went to my father and mother...'

The day she managed to return safely to her village and scuffle through the exhilarated crowds thronging to see the 'pride of their village', her eyes searched for two faces. She finally saw her parents quietly standing outside their thatched hut, with disbelief in their eyes and arms stretched out to embrace their heroic daughter.

Bachendri Pal was born as the third child to Kishan Singh Pal and Hansa Dei Negi of Nakuri village in Uttarakhand. The picturesque mountainous terrain of her village and her two brothers taking to mountaineering piqued her interest in the sport as a child. She says unabashedly of the rebellious child in her, 'As much as I loved my brothers, I resented the boys getting more attention and opportunities than us girls. I was determined not to take a back seat in the Pal family and to not only do what the boys did, but do it better.' This determination to climb over the barriers and biases, combined with the back-breaking physical tasks that any resident of hilly areas would end up doing for sheer survival, had already planted the seeds of India's first woman Everest climber in young Bachendri. At thirteen, when she had just completed her eighth standard, her father expressed anguish over his inability to send her to school to study further. She decided to fight the odds, and multi-tasked effectively by doing her share of exerting household chores, learnt tailoring and started rendering stitching services to village households in order to fund her higher education. In school, she excelled both in academics and outdoor sports, proving her exceptional abilities time and again.

Further, she chose to do a bachelor's degree in Sanskrit primarily due to her love for the Himalayas. She had known that the great poet of ancient India, Kalidasa, had made intriguing references to the Himalayas, which he called 'the measuring rod of the earth' in his *Kumarasambhava*. She thereby became the first woman graduate from her village and went on to do a Master's in Sanskrit and an additional degree which qualified her for a teaching job. By then, she knew that her heart lay in mountaineering and her eyes on the Everest top. She decided to take a course at the National Institute of Mountaineering, where her vice-principal, Major Prem Chand, had spotted the competence in her and even remarked 'Everest Material' in his report, declaring her as the best student of the course. When she received a letter in 1984, stating that she was selected for the Indian Mountaineering Foundation's Everest Expedition team, she was awestruck; she could not believe that she was ready for an Everest climb at that stage.

Much before all this unfurled, when she was a school girl, an incident ensured that her training towards becoming a mountaineer commenced right then. 'I remember the first time we had reached the snow line. I must have been about ten years old. It was a school group of ten—both boys and girls—who decided to climb the mountain on a Sunday morning. We walked and climbed higher and higher until we were at the foot of Gangotri glacier. We were thrilled at the feel of the crunchy snow

left
Bachendri Pal *(right)* and Arunima Sinha have proved to the world that there is no mountain beyond a determined mind's reach. Arunima considers Bachendri her strength and says, 'Bachendri realised my passion and determination and called me her *sherni* (lioness). She was one of my strongest supports in the entire journey.'

beneath our feet. We hadn't carried water in false expectation of finding some clear stream of water flowing through the hills. We ended up quenching our thirst with the snow, instead. Soon, it got cold and dark and we were left with no food or water. Since my brother and cousins knew that wild bears could attack us, we halted and made a partial overhead cover with branches. We kept a fire burning all night to keep wild animals away. It was only the next morning that we could begin the climb down, though we could barely walk. We suffered from extreme hunger, dehydration and fatigue. The air is rarefied at that height, making drinking water a must. Many felt giddy and began to vomit, yet we endured and that remains the singular adventure which sparked the mountain of interest in me.' Bachendri had tasted the excitement of climbing the mountains and nothing could hold her back.

Many prestigious awards, including the Padma Shri, Arjuna award, IMF gold medal of excellence and a place in the Guinness Book of Records have found their way to Bachendri's modest abode. Yet, what she considers to be the most rewarding aspect of her profession is that she has been able to impart her understanding of life and skills of mountaineering to the younger generation, especially young girls from rural areas. One such jewel in her crown is the proud owner of another 'first ever' achievement—Arunima Sinha—the first ever woman amputee to have scaled Mount Everest. If Bachendri's travails were arduous, Arunima's were deemed impossible, till she proved them all wrong.

Arunima, a former national-level volleyball player, is today the face of fortitude. She was twenty-three years old when life hurled shots at her in the form of some hooligans who attempted to rob her and mercilessly pushed her off a moving train when she was travelling from Lucknow to Delhi, in April 2011. On gaining consciousness, she found herself in a hospital bed, where the doctors told her that she had sustained multiple injuries on her legs and hips and in order to save her life, they had to perform a below-knee amputation on her left leg. It took some time for reality to sink in, but she braved it like none other.

On being asked what stoked her into dreaming of such a risky mission, she opens up, saying, 'It was out of sheer frustration. When I was in the hospital, everyone was worried for me, and I realised that I had to do something in my life so that people would stop looking at me with pity. When I read about scaling Mount Everest, I got inspired and spoke to my elder brother and my coach about it, and they encouraged me. So I decided to challenge myself. I turned my artificial leg into my strength and stubbornly chose the most difficult sport for myself. And I chased my dream with passion.' That is how, after eight long months in hospital, Arunima landed at Bachendri Pal's office at the Adventure Foundation and expressed her desire to be trained under her.

Bachendri was overtaken by the grit and gall that this young girl possessed, despite the adversities. She recollects that Arunima did not even have proper clothing to ensue training. She had lost her father at a young age and was supported by her working mother who also had to take care of the rest of the family. On being gifted a pair of lowers by the first Indian woman on Everest, Arunima beamed in gratitude and excitement. Bachendri said to her, 'I am giving it to the world's first physically challenged woman on the Everest.' Her words turned prophetic when the entire

right
Arunima Sinha trekking as a part of training. Being a socially sensitive person, she channels the money that she receives from awards and recognition, towards realising her dream of opening a sports academy for underprivileged and differently-abled people.

nation stood astounded at the unmatched feat of the girl with an iron will, a steely nerve and a prosthetic leg. The proud mentor declared on 21 May 2013, 'It's a moment of pride for the whole nation. The spirit, mental strength and will power of Arunima have been exemplary. She has defied all odds and will be an inspiration for millions throughout the world.' To that, the faithful pupil replied, 'Because Ma'am was with me, she believed in me, I could climb the Everest.'

Arunima's adventures at the precipice make for a chilling narrative in itself. It took fifty-two days of staunch courage and deep desire in her to battle the boulders and conquer the edgy peaks of snow. When she came back, she said she wished to dedicate her climb to 'those who lose hope' in their lives. Her dreams are beyond the reach of any sly plot of misfortune. She plans to start a sports academy in her home state of Uttar Pradesh and help physically challenged children realise their goals. Meanwhile, Bachendri wishes her student all the best in her endeavours.

Bachendri signs off with priceless words, 'While climbing a mountain, I discover myself and come to know more about me—what scares me, what worries me, how to boost my confidence and leverage my determination. To me, nature is not only a great teacher, but also a great purifier...it simplifies the problems, and purifies our paths. And life is worth living when you are on top of the world.'

—Divya S Iyer

Essence of a Woman

Sushmita Sen

A complete package, a nuance soul,
A delicate story, waiting to unfold...

The very womb of tales,
Generations will tell...

One who will assure the very core of existence,
Nurture life with absolute persistence,
Embrace love despite resistance...

Request God for such a powerful Omen,
He gently says...
She's called a 'Woman'.

—*Sushmita Sen*

Sushmita Sen is seen as one of the most successful single mothers in India. By adopting two children, Renee and Alisah, she has set an excellent example for adoption as well as raising girls independently. She is often called a 'rule-breaker' for the unconventional path she has chosen.

'Being a woman by itself is a gift of God, which all of us must appreciate. The origin of a child is a mother and a woman. A woman is the one who shares love and shows the man what love, caring, sharing is all about. That is the essence of a woman.' This was an eighteen-year-old Sushmita Sen's reply to a question that got her the Miss Universe 1994 crown. Two decades on, the young lady who was brought up in Air Force background lives and reiterates her belief about women.

She reminisces, 'During our time, there was no internet, so we didn't have access to answers or videos to refer to, of what winners of earlier pageants had said. We didn't go armed with coaching of all the knowledge that freely floats today. When I went on that stage, all I had was my upbringing in the Air Force environment and the desire to be someone.' Sushmita remembers how she chose not to use an interpreter and in hindsight feels that thanks to her limited English vocabulary, she could stick to exactly what she wanted to say and not fluff it up with intelligent words.

There has been an evolvement in the thought of what she now feels is the essence of a woman. 'By virtue of how nature defines her, the essence of a woman is that of a nurturer.' At thirty-eight, she is a mother of two adopted young girls Renee (fourteen), and Alisah (four) and is diversifying into a new business of creating brands, even as she is preparing to make a comeback in films after a four-year gap she took to raise Alisah. Being a single mother, she feels people look at her as a feminist, but she is far from it. She strongly believes that the male quotient in a relationship is equally important. She says, 'Despite the direction my life has taken, I strongly believe that the balance of nature dictates. There has to be a synergy of male and female energy and I appreciate both sides very much. But I also believe in the fact that out of the two, the woman gets to be the one who nourishes.'

At the young age of twenty-five, when her film career was flourishing, a lot of people were against her decision to adopt a child. 'I was very headstrong. After winning Miss Universe, as part of my CSR, I was taken to various orphanages. I had wanted to do something for kids since then. So I decided to start with one child. Meeting Mother Teresa before that had also influenced me a lot and I loved being with kids.'

She remembers that initially, when she took Renee home, it took some getting used to being a mother. Her parents had already told her that she would have to bring the child up on her own and they wouldn't be around to help her with it. Juggling shoots, events, press and taking care of the baby was quite a task. 'At first, it was very difficult, but once you find a rhythm with the child, you both fit into each other's life effortlessly. Having Renee taught me patience and was a good learning in being grounded. Before that, I had everything at my beck and call. But how can you instruct a baby to call you "ma" the first day she comes home or to start walking when you want her to walk?' she laughs.

She adds, 'Now Renee is fourteen and in a boarding school. She does not need me as much and the crises in her life are of a different kind. Alisah has grown up well, but she has asthma, so I need to take care of her. Having both of them taught me to love unconditionally. I am madly in love with my children, but don't obsess over them. I don't want them to make me proud. I just want them to hold tremendous pride in themselves. This I have learned from my experience with parenting.' While Renee was part and parcel of Sushmita's high profile public life, after Alisah came to her when she was one month old, she took a three years long break from acting and pursued running of the 'I Am She' brand, preparing and sending Indian women to the international pageant. 'It took less of my time and I didn't want to miss Alisah's formative years. I am glad I did that. I was creating that umbilical cord which didn't exist. Well meaning people told me that it was a wrong time to take a break to bring up a child, when I could use that time to concentrate on my film career, but I had set my priorities. I knew that I could come back and do well in films when I wanted to again, but would I get three years of my child's growing years back?'

Having been a product and part of the beauty and film industry, Sushmita understands that though the world would have us celebrate external beauty, it is the inner beauty that matters and is everlasting. Her suggestion to women world over is, 'If you go beyond limiting beauty by the length of your hair or parameters of your figure, you will find a beauty that's ethereal. Nature doesn't say wrinkles are ugly. Should I give up smiling—a thing that fills me with joy—just because I might get a few lines? My entire being celebrates when I am beaming with a smile. I am not going to give it up or be cautious of it to stay away from what is but a natural progression.'

She urges women to find beauty through their confidence and surround themselves with real people, who are supportive of who they are and are not around because of how they look. She believes that irrespective of one's shape or size, it's their confidence that attracts people towards them. 'I have seen so many men falling for and marrying women who may not fit the worldly perception of beauty. The cover may be beautiful, but if it lacks content, the book is useless.'

Few people know that when Sushmita was a child, she heard her parents bawling in front of their Texla B&W television set when they heard Squadron Leader Rakesh Sharma, the first Indian to travel in space say 'Saare jahan se achcha Hindustan humara' in response to Indira Gandhi's question on how India was looking from space. She asked her parents who he was, to which they told her that he was someone famous and the child decided that she would go on to become famous too. She didn't know how, but that became her dream. Ask her what she looks forward to today, since she has already achieved global success and she says, 'I saw success when I was very young. By virtue of that, you also see failure very young. I believe you must try everything. That experience makes you unafraid of failing. It teaches you that attempts fail. You don't. You stop associating yourself with 'I am a failure' or 'I am a success' tag. It's something that you did that was successful and something that you didn't that was not successful. When you learn these concepts so early in life, you explore avenues that most people would be very afraid to. I blew those cautions to the wind when I was very young. That is a plus. Life allows you a university to graduate from, where you are not graded against someone else.'

She sums up her ability to live life gracefully and on her terms to her practice of silence every day. She remembers finding the context of 'I Am' after which she has named her NGO and her company through the name of the forty-sixth deity of Kabbalah who is known as Elohim, which when translated into English means—I Am. 'I have been spiritual since childhood. The forty minutes I am in silence, I thank God, saying I am here right now. I am. I am happy…sad, anything I will attach to it later. It's very transitory. It will pass. As long as I am alive, I am. That doesn't change.'

right
Sushmita Sen celebrates Durga Puja, one of the biggest festivals on the Indian calendar. A devotee of Goddess Durga, who stands for courage and valour, Sushmita actively participates in the festivities by performing the Dhunuchi dance in Puja celebrations.

Sushmita reveals she taught her daughter a small prayer that she wrote herself. 'In Bengal, there is a saying whenever you feel anxious or fear in your chest and solar plexus—say "Dugga Dugga" (Goddess Durga). When she comes in, fear has to move out. Then you feel fearless. She represents courage.'

—Priyanka Jain

She Did Start the Fire

Harshini B Kanhekar, India's first fire woman

Harshini Kanhekar doing the Fire Tender Operator's role, as a part of a drill practice at her college. As a student, she was an enthusiastic cadet of the NCC Air Wing, where she engaged in several types of adventure activities like microlight flying, gliding, parasailing and aero-modelling.

right
Harshini Kanhekar during Squad Drill practice at the National Fire Service College in the year 2002.

S he didn't know that she would be the first woman in an Indian fire brigade, till she actually became one and created history. Being the first and the only female student in the fire-engineering course, she stunned everyone by her enrolment, endurance and stupendous performance at the National Fire Service College in Nagpur, Maharashtra—the only institution of its kind in India. 'It is a myth that women can't take as much physical strain as men,' Harshini B Kanhekar, the trail-blazing woman rightly points out, as she keenly keeps at her job at the Oil & Natural Gas Corporation of India.

'It was all quite interesting. Being the first woman in an all-male engineering course, no one knew what to look for in my medical test, as there were no criteria laid out specifically for women then. They just measured my height, weight and checked for colour-blindness,' she reminisces about her unusual decision to join the fire-engineering course at the NFSC. Harshini was already a science graduate then, but she realised that she had always nursed a secret penchant for uniformed jobs, right from her NCC (National Cadet Corps) days at school. Harshini decided to try to join the cadre of soldiers at the Indian Armed Defence Services, but in vain. Given her fondness for adventure sports and martial arts, it was no surprise that the twenty-three-year-old spunky woman applied for a course on fire engineering, at the suggestion of a friend who had spotted an advertisement in the newspaper that called for fire-fighters. And today, she says, 'I am in a very satisfied state of mind. I had wanted to be a soldier; and I am now very happy to be serving in Civil Defence.'

The days at NFSC were a dream of myriad shades, she recollects, 'I never missed a single session of training during the three-and-a-half-year period. While my male batch-mates were all residential students on the campus, I had no such privilege, as there was no women's hostel then.' Being a resident of Nagpur did help her overcome this inconvenience, yet commuting to and fro the college thrice daily for three years did take a toll on the fun-filled college life every student dreams of. Apart from studying a seemingly disparate set of subjects including applied psychology, town planning and rescue techniques, the course used to have drill sessions in the morning, classes in the afternoon and practical training sessions in the evening. Harshini had to put in extra efforts to see that she didn't falter. She was determined to live up to the expectations of her well-wishers, and prove those who looked at her rather curiously and wondered 'can she?' wrong.

And so she did, time and again proving her exceptional skills in instances that mandated a great deal of courage and physical strength. She is grateful to her seniors and instructors at the training centre, who did not treat her any differently from her peers. She received the same kind of training as the others, which included punishments of rigorous nature as well. But she never asked for consideration of any kind. She vividly remembers the incident that made her stand out when a difficult operation was being staged as a part of the drill training. 'We were required to lift a heavy dummy casualty on our shoulders from a high-rise building and climb down the ladder. When a team of four—including me—was falling in, the instructor asked me to fall out; and not knowing why, I was almost in tears. But to my surprise, soon after, he asked me to perform the task alone; I had the best chance to demonstrate my skills and prove myself.'

Lifting heavy appliances, performing dangerous tasks, logistical absurdities etc. were only a part of her struggle. Dealing with the patronising attitude of her peers, especially her male batch-mates, was even more complex. 'When the news of my enrolling into the fire-engineering course spread, the media had found its new woman champion. My male batch-mates could not stomach the fact that I was in the limelight, and that there was so much media attention on me. When one of them had wanted to be friends with me, the others booed him, because of which he had to help me on the sly. It hurt their male egos. In spite of my best efforts, they failed to realise that the attention was not on Harshini Kanhekar per se, but on the first woman would-be fire engineer.' This resulted in them boycotting her, so much so that she used to dread those ten-minute breaks during their drills, when she

would find herself side-lined and left to herself. But she managed to get over her immediate loneliness by perusing her slam-book and reminding herself of the fact that those were small thorns on her way and that she could tackle them all, with the bigger goal leading the way.

More exciting experiences were underway, as she continued with her field training. While working at Laxmi Nagar Fire Station in New Delhi, she had to attend calls and plunge into appropriate action in a matter of minutes, even at the dead of night; once again being the only female member of the team. The ungodly hours, the lack of women in her company, the panic situation that any fire accident would give rise to—none of these stifled her. In fact, it only added more fibre to her steely nerve.

So where did she acquire the bravado from? 'I think it is all due to my upbringing. I give the credit to my parents,' says Harshini modestly. She fondly remembers her childhood days with her elder brother and sister, who were all given equal opportunity and wide exposure. In the era when women struggled to pursue their own interests, her father Bapurao Kanhekar, who was a civil engineer by profession, took keen interest in seeing that her mother Maya Kanhekar, completed her higher education and became a graduate. Harshini confesses that the proudest moment in her life was seeing her father flash her NFSC ID card in great pride and contentment, which gave her study at NFSC a much deeper meaning. It is not without reason that Harshini insists that her name be written in full, with the initials of her father, as Harshini B Kanhekar. Her mother cannot contain her happiness even after a decade since Kanhekar graduated from NFSC. 'She has made us so proud,' quivers her mother over the phone, from her Nagpur abode.

In 2006, Harshini was selected as the first woman fire and security officer at ONGC, through a campus recruitment drive at her college. She was fortunate enough to receive encouragement and exposure aplenty from her seniors at ONGC. 'In my very first posting at Mehsana, Gujarat, dotted with oil and gas wells, I was assigned field duty, which was a twenty-four hour on-call fire related job. Our scope was the entire Mehsana district. Being a small place with hardly any fire stations on its roll, ONGC would pitch in to address civic emergencies as well. Consequently, I attended to emergencies like eruptions of oil and gas as well as domestic fire. I, thus, got great experiences in dousing fire,' says Kanhekar.

Currently, she is based at ONGC, Mumbai and involved with off-shore drilling services. Kanhekar attributes her success to her boss, Kalyanbrata Roy, GM (Drilling), ONGC, Mumbai region, for the encouragement he has given her. At his behest, she is sent to do fire-related enquiries and inspections at its rigs. 'I have not received any complaint from anyone. So, I think in the future too, we will give such opportunities to suitable female candidates. She is lucky to be in a company that has its own human resources and hence does not hire manpower from outside. Because in that case, things could have become more gender-biased,' explains Roy.

Though she still cherishes her fondness for the uniform unabashedly, once she is out of her ring of fire, Harshini is very much a cheerful young woman who loves to party, indulge in good food—her favourite being the Barbeque Nation chain of restaurants—and enjoys watching MTV Roadies. A music lover with particular fascination for string instruments, Kanhekar is a romantic at heart, what with her

choice of films—the Hindi romantic musical, *Dilwale Dulhaniya Le Jayenge* to the Hollywood epic *Titanic*. She has done a short-term course in cinematography and dreams of directing some day; the setting for a short movie revolving around a domesticated dog is already on her mind. The pin-board at her office sports a portrait of her three-year old Labrador, Sessy. And thanks to NCC, she is still into trekking and biking, and owns a bike and a jeep.

Anyone who meets her would appreciate the sense of contentment in her life. She loves her job, believes that the future of her career is bright, owns a modest two-bedroom apartment in Khandeshwer near Mumbai, and regularly commutes between Mumbai and Nagpur where her family lives, where it all began, where she did start the fire. Ask her if the feeling of being the first Indian woman fire engineer has sunk in, and she says rather candidly, 'Yes, I am aware, and happy about the fact that women have one more career to opt for. But if you ask me, my dream for Indian women—I want each of us to get our due space.'

—Sudeshna Chatterjee

Harshini Kanhekar during a fire-fighting drill in Nagpur. Despite being the only woman in her sphere of activity, she was given equal opportunities at every step, and her skills prospered under unbiased guidance.

KADAMBINI
GANGULY

India's first woman graduate in medicine, Kadambini Ganguly was a perfect example of matching professionalism with personal and family responsibilities. American historian David Kopf wrote about Kadambini, 'Her ability to rise above circumstances and to realise her potential as a human being made her a prize attraction to her community, dedicated ideologically to the liberation of women.' Kadambini was among the first women college graduates in India and one of the first Asian women doctors.

Born to Brahmo parents in 1861, Kadambini became the first woman to enter the University of Calcutta, in 1878. With her and another woman student, Chandramukhi Basu, began the process in India of letting women into modern colleges and today thousands of women study in hundreds of universities in the country. After graduating from Bethune College, Kadambini joined Calcutta Medical College and she and Anandi Gopal Joshi became India's first women physicians.

Her achievement was especially noteworthy as she studied medicine after she got married and became a mother, looking after a large family. Recommending Kadambini for a post at the Lady Dufferin hospital, Florence Nightingale wrote to a friend in 1888, 'Do you know or could tell me anything about Mrs Ganguly? After she made up her mind to become a doctor, has had one, if not two children since. But she was absent only thirteen days for her lying-in! And did not miss, I believe, a single lecture!'

Kadambini and her husband were involved in movements for suffrage and women's rights, social philanthropy and political activism. They were actively involved in efforts to improve work conditions of female coal miners in eastern India. Kadambini also worked towards improvement of work conditions of women labourers in the tea gardens of Assam. Soon after the foundation of the Indian National Congress in 1885, she demanded the right for women's representation at the annual sessions. Theosophist Annie Besant applauded Kadambini for being 'a symbol that India's freedom would uplift India's womanhood'.

Kadambini was also among the first Indian women to go to Europe to pursue higher studies, in 1892. She returned with three advanced degrees in medicine and surgery and became a well-known doctor. She died in 1923.

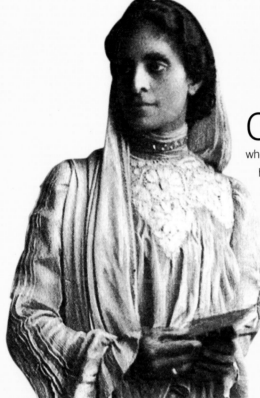

CORNELIA
SORABJI

Cornelia Sorabji became India's first woman barrister in 1924, after passing out from the bar at Lincoln's Inn, where she was admitted in 1922. She had, however, begun her fight for the rights of women, and education of children from 1894, taking it upon herself to stand up against the purdah system, an old custom that prohibited women from showing their faces to men outside of their families. She became an advocate for hundreds of veiled women.

Cornelia had started petitioning the India Office, to grant a female advisor for representing women and children in provincial courts, twenty years before she was allowed to officially practice in courts. In 1904, she was chosen as the Lady Assistant to the Court of Wards of and by 1907, she was also appointed in the provinces of Bengal, Bihar, Orissa, and Assam. During the next twenty years of her service as a lawyer, it is estimated that she helped over six hundred women and orphans.

Born in Nashik, into a large Parsi family in 1866, Cornelia was educated both at home and at mission schools. She was the first female graduate from Bombay University and in 1892 became the first woman to study law at and graduate from the Oxford University, thus becoming the first Indian national to study at any British university. Later, she also became the first Indian woman to practice law in Britain and India.

Cornelia led a very interesting life, experiencing two extreme environments, one where the British ruled over India and the other where the nation positioned itself as a free country. As a woman, she was able to bring about major changes in the legal system. Her most lasting contribution was, perhaps, that she brought women out of their homes, creating rules for women's markets, shopping days, by sending some to literacy camps and sending others to train as nurses and teachers.

She wrote a book about several of her cases, called, *Between the Twilight*. It is acknowledged that she contributed to *Queen Mary's Book of India,* 1943, which featured authors like TS Elliot and Dorothy L Sayers. She died in 1954. In 2012, her bust was unveiled at Lincoln's Inn.

KAMALADEVI
CHATTOPADHYAY

Many of the nation's premier institutions, like the Sangeet Natak Akademi, the National School of Drama and the Crafts Council of India, were set up at Kamaladevi Chattopadhyay's initiative.

Kamaladevi inherited her independent and scholarly spirits from the women of the Saraswat Brahmin family she was born into in 1903. She went on to study in India and abroad. Due to Partition, thousands were displaced from the western frontiers of the country, and Kamaladevi jumped into rehabilitation work in 1947, setting up the Indian Cooperative Union, a body that facilitated the growth of the cooperative township of Faridabad on Delhi's outskirts, where Kamaladevi managed to return to 50,000 refugees their lives and livelihoods. It was while engaged in this work that Kamaladevi realised, how the British model of factory-produced goods had slowly killed India's traditional art and craftwork that rural families engage in.

From helping refugee women sell embroidery and lace-work, Kamiladevi's attention soon moved to the rest of the country. Before independence, one did not see the Thanjavur Bommai as decorative household items, a pat painting on the walls and a chuktu carpet on the floor or wear the angami naga, lac bangles and tilla jutis. Kamaladevi, sporting bright Madurai cotton saris and ethnic jewellery, changed the way everyday India looks at beauty. Through the Crafts Council of India, Kamaladevi brought dignity and life to the households of millions of Indian artisans, who have today emerged to contribute to an incredible brand India. She single-handedly managed to transform the indigenous textile sector that had been shrouded for two centuries by the European mill-cloth. National School of Drama has given a platform for expression of the most modern of creative theatre as well as for the revival of India's grand epics.

Kamaldevi was awarded Padma Vibhushan in 1984. No wonder, President R Venkataraman said, 'Flower buds seemed to blossom at her touch—whether they be flower buds of human beings or institutions. People became more human and more sensitive to the deeper impulses of society when they came into contact with her...' Kamaladevi passed away in 1988. She was a cherished institution herself, leaving on modern India her stamp of vitality that makes India more vibrant today.

RUKMINI DEVI
ARUNDALE

Rukmini Devi reinvented the Bharatanatyam dance form. She was also known as 'Pranimitra', an ardent advocate of animal rights. Rukmini Arundale was also the woman who first gave space in India to the German Montessori method of educating tiny tots in the 1940s and created the cultural repository, Kalakshetra Foundation, which today is a deemed university, known worldwide not only for dance and music, but for conserving traditions of printing like 'Kalamkari'.

Rukmini Devi Arundale was born in 1904, into a family deeply influence by the Theosophical Movement. While on a world-tour with her husband, British Theosophist George Arundale, the young and beautiful Rukmini met the famed Russian ballerina Anna Pavlova and inspired by Pavlova, began to seriously learn dancing. Pavlova told her not to get carried away by ballet, but instead, to search for the dance traditions in India and bring these to centre stage.

Sadhir, the traditional temple dance of Tamil Nadu, was waiting to be given a new lease of life. It was a socially frowned upon activity until Rukmini Devi learnt it and gave the first public performance by a Brahmin woman. In the following years, after the temple servitude system was abolished, she brought noted performers as teachers to Kalakshetra, the institute George and she had set up. Among Kalakshetra students are well known dancers like Sarada Hoffman, Sanjukta Panigrahi, Yamini Krishnamurti and Leela Samson. From *Ramayana* to Kalidas' *Kumarasambhavam* and Jaidev's *Gita Govindam*, Rukmini Arundale danced in and choreographed exquisite performances. She also danced in a movie called *Raja Desingh*.

The Kalakshetra Foundation also facilitated Maria Montessori's first kindergarten, and a middle and a high school in Annie Besant's memory. It also housed animal care shelters and organisations like the Blue Cross. Rukmini Devi steered The Prevention of Cruelty to Animals Act, 1960 and set up the Animal Welfare Board of India two years later. This Padma Bhushan award winner and two-term Rajya Sabha member died in 1986, leaving behind a legacy that would be difficult for any one individual to emulate.

HOMAI
VYARWALLA

Homai Vyarwalla was India's first woman photojournalist, whose work until 1970 not only captured the last days of the British Raj in India but drew a picture of the birth and growth of a new nation—a free India progressing through the first three decades of trials and triumphs.

Born into a Parsi family in Navsari, Gujarat in 1913, Homai grew up in Mumbai, graduating from the Sir JJ School of Fine Arts. She began photographing in the 1930s, inspired by her husband Manekshaw. Her professional career began with World War II, when she began working for the British Information Service in Delhi in 1942.

At BIS, Homai worked in near anonymity, the field of photography dominated then by Western photojournalists such as Henri Cartier-Bresson and Margaret Bourke-White. Quietly, she went about photographing many politicians, including Mahatma Gandhi, Jawaharlal Nehru, Jinnah and Sardar Patel. Homai also shot the meeting of the Congress Working Committee that sanctioned the decision to partition India. Among her more significant contributions was the photo of the first Flag-hoisting at the Red Fort on 15 August 1947. She recorded the departure of the last Viceroy, Lord Mountbatten, from the country and the funerals of Gandhi, Nehru and Lal Bahadur Shastri. Homai was a fearless and adventurous woman. Once left stranded in Sikkim, after taking images of a young Dalai Lama crossing the border in 1959, she hitched a ride back on an army truck.

'I didn't know these images I was taking were that important till after fifty years since I started work, when people started asking for them,' Homai told her biographer, Sabeena Gadihoke. 'My first images were of a picnic of a women's club in Mumbai. I was paid one rupee for each photo.' In 2010, Homai handed over her entire collection of prints, negatives, cameras and other memorabilia to a Delhi-based foundation for safekeeping and documentation. Homai's work was recognised with India's first National Photo Award for Lifetime Achievement in 2010 and the Padma Vibhushan in 2011. She died in 2012.

LAKSHMI SEHGAL

Captain Lakshmi is best remembered as the freedom fighter who fought the Allied Forces during World War II as the head of the women's wing of Netaji Subhash Chandra Bose's Indian National Army. Yet she lived most part of her life as a compassionate doctor, who selflessly worked for the upliftment of the poor, long past her ninety summers.

Lakshmi Swaminathan was born in 1914, in a lawyer's family in Madras. She earned an MBBS degree from the Madras Medical College in 1938. In 1940, Lakshmi set up a clinic in Singapore, where she provided medical help to the poor and to migrant Indians, establishing herself as an extremely compassionate and competent doctor. When Singapore surrendered to the Japanese, Lakshmi took care of wounded Indian prisoners of war. It was meeting Subhash Chandra Bose that brought a radical change in her life. Subhash chose her to lead his long-planned women's contingent, which they decided to call the 'Rani of Jhansi Regiment'. She received a tremendous response from women who were eager to join the all-women regiment. That is where she got the title of Captain. Working with the Indian National Army, she began the march to Burma in December 1944. She was arrested by the British and kept in Rangoon as a prisoner till 1946.

After her release, she devoted herself to the rehabilitation of imprisoned and de-mobbed INA personnel. She worked with refugees from divided India and helped in their rehabilitation. In 1971, Lakshmi organised relief camps and arranged for medical help in Kolkata, to look after the refugees coming from Bangladesh.

Lakshmi Sehgal was also extremely active in politics, first in the trade union and then the women's movement. She joined the Communist Party of India (M) and represented it in the Rajya Sabha. She was one of the founding members of the All India Democratic Women's Association, a premier women's organisation. In 1998, Lakshmi Sehgal was awarded the Padma Vibhushan and was a presidential candidate for the Left parties in 2002. Captain Lakshmi passed away in 2012.

MS SUBBULAKSHMI

Thava suprabhatham aravinda lochane
Bhavathu prasanna mukha chandra mandale
Vidhisankarendra vanitha bhirarchithe
Vrishasaila natha davithel daya nidhe

There could be no greater glory for a singer than to have her musical hymns, the *Venkateswara Suprabhatam*, sung every morning at the Tirupati temple to wake up Lord Balaji. Or for that matter, sing at Mahatma Gandhi's request, *Vaishnava Janato or Hari Tuma Haro*. For the renowned Carnatic musician M S Subbulakshmi, this was a natural progression in a career that brought not only name and fame but also coveted awards like the Bharat Ratna—the first for a singer. She was also awarded the Padma Vibhushan and Ramon Magsaysay Award. A Kancheevaram sari shade known as MS Blue is named after her and to mark her ninety-seventh birth anniversary, Google had a doodle.

Popularly referred to as MS, Subbulakshmi was born in 1916, into a family of temple musicians in Madurai. She grew up surrounded by music and her first public performance was at age eleven, in the hundred-pillar hall inside the Ucchi Pillayar temple in Tiruchirapalli. Her first gramophone recording was done when she was just ten years old. The songs were *Maragatavadivu* and *Oothukuzhiyinile* in an impossibly high pitch. By the time she was thirteen, she was performing at the prestigious Madras Music Academy. Subbulakshmi soon became one of the leading Carnatic vocalists of the times. She had begun touring the world for concerts by the time she was seventeen. Her concerts were held at the Edinburgh International Festival of Music and Drama in 1963, the Carnegie Hall, the UN General Assembly in 1966, the Royal Albert Hall in 1982 and the Festival of India in Moscow in 1987.

Subbulakshmi also acted in several Tamil films, but it was her title roles in the Tamil and Hindi (1947) rendition of the film, *Meera*, that made her famous throughout the country and earned her the name Saint-Singer. She popularised Annamacharya kirtans and ragas like Shankarabharanam and Kambhoji. She also sang songs penned by Chandrasekarendra Saraswati, the 69th pontiff of the Kanchi Sankara Mutt. The golden-voiced Subbulakshmi died in 2004. There is a commemorative postage stamp on her.

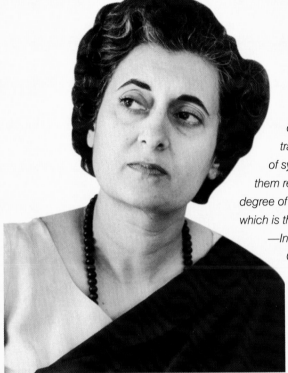

INDIRA GANDHI

To be liberated, woman must feel free to be herself, not in rivalry to man but in the context of her own capacity and her personality. Indian women are traditionally conservative but they also have the genius of synthesis, to adapt and to absorb. That is what gives them resilience to face suffering and to meet upheavals with a degree of calm, to change constantly and yet remain changeless, which is the quality of India herself.
—Indira Gandhi, speaking at an All-India Women's Conference event in 1980.

Indira Priyadarshini Gandhi, the 'Woman of the Millennium', was India's first woman prime minister and one of recent history's most charismatic leaders. Born in 1917, she had a lonely childhood in an affluent household, in company of an ailing mother, Kamala Nehru and a distant father, Jawaharlal, a freedom fighter mostly in jail, who would communicate largely by writing to her. About her father's letters, she later wrote, '...they were not merely letters to be read and put away. They brought a fresh outlook and aroused a concern for people and interest in the world around. They taught one to treat nature as a book. I spent absorbing hours studying stones and plants, the life of insects and at night, the stars.' She was afraid of darkness, cooked on slow fire so that the colours of vegetables were retained, she loved crosswords and was an excellent storyteller, her biographers say.

She was elected president of the Indian National Congress Party in 1959 and became Prime Minister in 1966. Her tenure till 1977 saw India change from a nation dependent on food aid to a self-sufficient country. Indira Gandhi steered the nationalisation of banks and oil companies, her grant programmes had eradication of poverty or *Garibi Hatao* as agitprop. Indira also took the diplomatically tough call to test India's first nuclear weapon in 1967 and space exploration. During her regime, the kingdom of Sikkim became a part of India and in 1971, Bangladesh became a free country. After a massive electoral victory in 1971, Indira became Prime Minister for a second term. She won a third term as Prime Minister in 1980.

'I am alive today, I may not be there tomorrow. I shall continue to serve till my last breath and when I die every drop of my blood will strengthen India and keep a united India alive,' Indira Gandhi said, the day before she died on 30 October 1984.

AMRITA PRITAM

Me—a book in the attic.
Maybe some covenant or hymnal.
Or a chapter from the *Kama Sutra*,
or a spell for intimate afflictions.
But then it seems I am none of these.
(If I were, someone would have read me.)
  Sometimes I think to catch the scent—
      what lies in my future?
        Worry makes my binding come off.
        —Amrita Pritam (translated from the Punjabi by DH Tracy and Mohan Tracy)

This daughter of Punjab from Gujranwala lived by her words, which often raised eyebrows, but they are words that continue to be cherished by readers. A writer's best trophy is that he or she is known by her writing and Amrita Pritam's writings have been translated in English, Albanian, Bulgarian, French, Polish, Russian, Spanish, Danish and Japanese and twenty-one Indian languages. Her literary corpus includes seventy-five books, of which there are twenty-eight novels, eighteen volumes of verse, five short stories and sixteen other prose compositions.

Born in 1919, Amrita Pritam straddled the cusp of history, growing up in turbulent times which culminated in the dividing of a nation. Living in pre-Partition Lahore, Amrita gave expression to her loneliness through a first anthology, *Amrit Lehran* (Immortal Waves), published in 1936. On love at sixteen, Amrita wrote: 'Came my sixteenth year—like a stranger. Inside me, there was an awareness I could not explain...Like a thief, came my sixteenth year, stealthily like a prowler in the night, stealing in through the open window at the head of my bed...'

By 1943 began her transition from a romantic poet to a novelist painting the image of social realities of the times. Her elegy to Waris Shah, the eighteenth century Sufi poet, shot her to fame as a writer. The story of migration came in Amrita Pritam's most acclaimed novel, *Pinjar* (The Skeleton, 1950), and was made into an award-winning film in 2003. In India, Amrita became involved with the Progressive Writers' Movement. In 1955 came her collection of poems *Sunehra* (Messages) and she became the first woman recipient of the prestigious Sahitya Akademi Award. She was awarded Padma Vibhushan in 2004. Amrita Pritam left this world in her sleep in 2005.

CB MUTHAMMA

India's first woman diplomat, Chonira Belliappa Muthamma, mentored some of India's important peace and disarmament resolutions, steered gender justice in workplace and wrote popular books analysing systems. She maintained, 'This country has that human, intangible dimension that makes India so truly beautiful, so tangible and material, yet so spiritually rich and resourceful.'

She will be best remembered for her tireless crusade to establish gender equality in the then male dominated Indian civil services. Today, roughly one out of six Foreign Service officers in India are women and India has since then seen three women foreign secretaries, apart from several others who have successfully rendered most difficult of assignments.

Born in 1924, in the picturesque hill town of Madikeri, the feisty Muthamma did her schooling in Kodagu and then did an MA in English Literature from Presidency College, Chennai. In 1949, she joined the Foreign Service, remaining in the IFS for thirty-two years, rising to the rank of an ambassador. After a stint in Paris, Muthamma was chosen as India's representative to the Independent Commission on Disarmament and Security Issues, set up by then Swedish Prime Minister Olaf Palme. This was the famous 1986 six-nation collaboration under UN aegis, in which the Rajiv Gandhi Action Plan for total disarmament and peace was formulated. Muthamma was the key support mechanism for the Indian negotiations, when India and Russia signed a 'Joint Declaration of Principles of a Nuclear-Weapon-Free and Non-Violent World', echoing effort toward complete disarmament, elimination of nuclear weapons and progress toward a 'nuclear-weapon free civilisation'.

The same hands that drafted strongly-worded international treaties that still hold good, wrote delightful books like, *The Essential Kodava Cookbook*. Muthamma also came up with a bestseller that continues to be relevant even today, *Slain by the System: India's Real Crisis*. She gave fifteen acres of land in Delhi to the Missionaries of Charity. Muthamma died in 2009, leaving an inheritance of work parity for India's 115 million female workforce.

Come, Be my Light

Mother Teresa

The hallowed land of India has beckoned many a compassionate soul from across the seas. They seek to soak in her sacred spirit of faith and belief, and dedicate their lives in the service of humanity. Amongst those whose contributions have transcended geographical boundaries, some continue to make their presence felt by the lasting nature of their actions.

Sister Nivedita (1867-1911), as Swami Vivekananda rechristened her, was born Margeret Elizabeth Noble in Ireland, and made Calcutta her home to fulfil her mission. Blanche Rachel Mirra Alfassa (1878-1973), who was born in Paris, went on to become The Mother at the Aurobindo Ashram in Pondicherry, being the spiritual disciple of Shri Aurobindo. Madeline Slade (1892-1982), a British woman who was endearingly called Miraben by Indians, was Mahatma Gandhi's disciple and devoted her life to the promotion of Gandhian ideology. Clearly, they had all been inspired by a revered Indian persona whose luminous messages reverberated across the globe, attracted sensitive souls in quest of truth and accepted them wholeheartedly into the nation's own philosophical narrative. India has, thus, blessed many adopted daughters, who have become her own.

Among such illustrious daughters of India, the life and deeds of Mother Teresa clearly stand out, for she brought with her a new covenant—the covenant of prayer, a new charter—the charter for compassion and a new gift—the gift of love and care. She was a crusader for the needs of the unwanted, unloved and uncared for.

Born as Agnes Gonxha Bojaxhiu in Skopje, Macedonia, on 26 August 1910, she lost her father at the tender age of eight. Her mother, Drane, had an undeniably significant role in instilling rocklike faith in young Agnes. At the age of twelve, she felt the call of God, to serve in his light, which sustained through her teenage years. At the age of eighteen, she was driven by the intense desire to become a missionary of God and joined the order of Sisters of Loreto in Ireland and came to be called Sister Mary Teresa. After a few months of training in Ireland, Sister Teresa came to India in 1929, where she took her vows formally as a nun in 1931, in the city of Calcutta. After taking her Final Profession of Vows, she came to be known as Mother Teresa. She moulded minds and honed the intellect of the young girls at the St Mary's Convent school in Calcutta from 1932 to 1946 as a teacher and subsequently as the principal.

The transformational moment in her life occurred on 10 September 1946, while she was undertaking a train journey from Calcutta to Darjeeling for her annual retreat. She is said to have received divine inspiration from Jesus. He revealed to her the desire of His heart and instructed her thus: 'Come, be My light...and radiate His love on souls.' She followed His desire and founded the Missionaries of Charity on 17 August 1948, in a temporary lodging at the Little Sisters of the Poor in Calcutta, which gradually blossomed into a garden of love spreading the fragrance of charity and care, the world over. Ever since, her hands held the burden of physical pain even as her voice hummed the song of divine love.

A diminutive woman, dressed in a white sari with a blue border drawn over her head is an enduring image in the heart of every modern Indian. The day she set out to visit the slums of Calcutta, she embarked on a life-long endeavour to bring smiles on the faces of human beings deprived of love and care. Her overarching humility revealed itself to an entire generation that heard her say thus on 10 December 1979, after receiving the Nobel Peace Prize, 'The poor are very wonderful people. One evening we went out and we brought home four people from the street. And one of them was in a most terrible condition, and I told the Sisters: You take care of the other three, I will take care of this one that looks worse. So I did for her all that my love can do. I put her in bed, and there was such a beautiful smile on her face. She took hold of my hand, as she said one word only: Thank you, and she died. I could not help but examine my conscience before her, and I asked what would I say if I was in her place. And my answer was very simple. I would have tried to draw a little attention to myself, I would have said I am hungry, that I am dying, I am cold, I am in pain, or something, but she gave me much more—she gave me her grateful love. And she died with a smile on her face.' Today the Missionaries of Charity has over 6000 sisters from the 610 foundations in 123 countries of the world, working relentlessly to infuse love, care and dignity in the lives of innumerable men and women marred by pain, agony and suffering.

After having travelled far and wide in order to pursue her extraordinary mission of charity, Mother Teresa spent the final weeks of her life in Calcutta with the people whose lives had by then become her own. She breathed her last on 5 September 1997. Within two years, the Vatican beatified her as a saint in real life; and she lives on ever since as the Blessed Mother Teresa, as a candle that sheds the light of hope and melts selflessly in service of the needy. Her invincible courage, infallible conviction and intense faith has left behind a legacy of caring and sharing, like never before. 'By blood, I am Albanian. By citizenship, an Indian. By faith, I am a Catholic nun. As to my calling, I belong to the world', saying thus Mother Teresa remains an eternal source of hope and inspiration to many an Indian rendering a universal meaning to the timeless Sanskrit phrase Vasudaiva Kutumbakam—The World is My Family.

—Divya S Iyer

Photograph Credits

Front Cover: Rukmini Centenary volume

Pg ii: Sanjay Austa

Pg iv & v: AFP/Getty Images

Pg vi & vii: Confluence Pictures

Pg ix: UN Photo/Christopher Herwig

Pg xi: Boisvieux Christophe/Hemis/Corbis

Pg xii: AFP/Getty Images

Pg xii: Getty Images

Pg xiii: Getty Images

Pg xiii: Getty Images

Pg 1: UIG via Getty Images

Pg 3: AFP/Getty Images

Pg 5 & 6: Biocon

Pg 7: Bettmann/CORBIS

Pg 9: Bhanu Athaiya

Pg 10: AFP/Getty Images

Pg 11: Air India/Bhanu Athaiya

Pg 12: AFP/Getty Images

Pg 13: Shahnaz Husain

Pg 16: Getty Images

Pg 16: Sanjay Austa

Pg 17: Sunita Narain

Pg 20: FlickrVision

Pg 21: Jacqueline M. Koch/Corbis

Pg 23: Bloomberg via Getty Images

Pg 26: Bloomberg via Getty Images

Pg 28: India Today Group/Getty Images

Pg 28: Hindustan Times via Getty Images

Pg 29: Augustus Binu/
www.dreamsparrow.net/
Wikimedia Commons

Pg 32: Philippe Lissac/ /Photononstop/
Corbis

Pg 32: Hindustan Times via Getty Images

Pg 33: Pallava Bagla/Corbis

Pg 35: Padma Bandopadhyay

Pg 36: Padma Bandopadhyay

Pg 37: Stringer/Xinhua Press/Corbis

Pg 38: AFP/Getty Images

Pg 39: Getty Images

Pg 42: India Today Group/Getty Images

Pg 43: AFP/Getty Images

Pg 46: Sanjay Austa

Pg 47: MC Mary Kom

Pg 48: MC Mary Kom

Pg 50: MC Mary Kom

Pg 52: AFP/Getty Images

Pg 53: UIG via Getty Images

Pg 55: Ela R Bhatt

Pg 57: Hugh Sitton/Corbis

Pg 59: Susheela Bhan

Pg 60: Altaf Zargar/ZUMA Press/Corbis

Pg 62:Blaine Harrington III/Corbis

Pg 64: Altaf Zargar/ZUMA Press/Corbis

Pg 64: Alison Wright/Corbis

Pg 65: AFP/Getty Images

Pg 68: Nevil Zaveri

Pg 69: Sphoorthi Theatre/Teejan Bai

Pg 71: Sphoorthi Theatre/Teejan Bai

Pg 72: India Today Group/Getty Images

Pg 73: Lo Ping Fai/Xinhua Press/Corbis

Pg 75: Yue Yuewei/Xinhua Press/Corbis

Pg 76: AFP/Getty Images

Pg 77: Pallava Bagla/Corbis

Pg 78: Pallava Bagla/Corbis

Pg 80: Pallava Bagla/Corbis

Pg 80: AFP/Getty Images

Pg 81 & 82: Pallava Bagla/Corbis

Pg 83: Chandro Tomar

Pg 86: AFP/Getty Images

Pg 86: AFP/Getty Images

Pg 87: Alisha Abdullah

Pg 89: Alisha Abdullah

Pg 90: Getty Images

Pg 91: Arunima Sinha

Pg 94: Arunima Sinha

Pg 95: India Today Group/Getty Images

Pg 98: India Today Group/Getty Images

Pg 99: Harshini B Kanhekar

Pg 100: Harshini B Kanhekar

Pg 102: Harshini B Kanhekar

Pg 113: Jean-Louis Atlan/Sygma/Corbis